Setting
Jesus
Free

Lessons From Luke

First published by O Books, 2009
O Books is an imprint of John Hunt Publishing Ltd., The Bothy, Deershot Lodge, Park Lane, Ropley,
Hants, SO24 0BE, UK
office1@o-books.net
www.o-books.net

Distribution in:

UK and Europe
Orca Book Services
orders@orcabookservices.co.uk
Tel: 01202 665432 Fax: 01202 666219   Int.
code (44)

USA and Canada
NBN
custserv@nbnbooks.com
Tel: 1 800 462 6420 Fax: 1 800 338 4550

Australia and New Zealand
Brumby Books
sales@brumbybooks.com.au
Tel: 61 3 9761 5535 Fax: 61 3 9761 7095

Far East (offices in Singapore, Thailand,
Hong Kong, Taiwan)
Pansing Distribution Pte Ltd
kemal@pansing.com
Tel: 65 6319 9939 Fax: 65 6462 5761

South Africa
Stephan Phillips (pty) Ltd
Email: orders@stephanphillips.com
Tel: 27 21 4489839 Telefax: 27 21 4479879

Text copyright John Churcher 2008

Design: Stuart Davies

ISBN: 978 1 84694 249 5

A CIP catalogue record for this book is available
from the British Library.

Printed by Digital Book Print

Setting
Jesus
Free

Lessons From Luke

John Churcher

BOOKS

Winchester, UK
Washington, USA

CONTENTS

Foreword

As with all empires, they will pass away. The Egyptian Empire lasted over 3000 years, but it went. The three dynasties of the Babylonian Empire lasted, off and on, some 2000 years, but it went. The Roman Empire lasted 1200 years, but it went. The British Empire lasted less than 500 years, but it went. The Empire of the Soviet Union lasted 70 years, but it went. The Empire of the US dollar has been the international reserve currency for the last 60 years, but it will go. And the Empire of Christianity, known as Christendom, that started with Constantine and his vision before the battle of Milvian Bridge, has lasted almost 1800 years, but it is going and unless there are changes to its traditional and comforting teachings, Bible interpretations and Creeds and doctrines, it will pass into history like all the other Empires. But somehow, we have to set Jesus free from the institutional Church constraints of both the past and the present so that there is a future for his values and teachings.

I have come late into the ordained ministry of the Christian Church with a three-fold mission. The first is to support those already in the Church, whether or not they agree with my theology, but I want to encourage people to think outside of the traditional boxes of faith and their inherited understandings of God. Every action has a reaction, and some Church members agree with my theology and some do not. But every inaction also has a reaction, and my fear for the Church and the message of Jesus is such that there is no future for either unless we drag our heads out of the sands of tradition, fundamentalism and literalism, and face faith with what we have discovered in all the 'isms' of modern and post-modern life.

Secondly, I want to bridge the gap again between those who once belonged but have turned their back on the Church – owing to the perceived irrelevance of traditional teachings – no longer able to belong while being intellectually dishonest to themselves and to their fellow Christian pilgrims. And the third challenge is that of the evangelist, to gently confront the people who have no active faith involvement or no experience of the Church but who so easily reject that which they do not know!

This book is not so much a commentary on Luke's Gospel – many eminent scholars have done this already. It is more a study of Luke's Gospel seen through the eyes of a Christian minister who is seeking after a relevant Spiritual Truth based upon contemporary Biblical scholarship concerning the radical message from a radical Messenger, or as my Hindu friends say, another Manifestation of the One God, Jesus of Nazareth.

This book is based upon sermons that were preached over a 6-month period or so. In the style of many preachers, ideas and themes will repeat themselves. Repetition in the pulpit is usually acceptable to the listeners, and, hopefully, repetition in a book will not cause too many problems for the reader.

Through its pages I attempt to explore the fresh expressions and insights of the Jesus Seminar-kind of scholarship into that which we call 'God', and to challenge afresh our way of life and understanding of God in the post-modern world in which we now operate. 'God' is not a name. It a three letter word attempting to describe 'Whatever' is within, about and beyond; whatever we may call the 'transcendent and the imminent'. Human language can never define whatever it is that some call 'Ground of All Being', 'Eternal Sacred', 'Spirit of Life' and a myriad other names. We only have human language to try to describe an experience of that which is always 'More Than' and human language is never sufficient for the task. Therefore I will use the word 'God' as shorthand for a set of eternal principles, including Perfect, Sacrificial and Unconditional Love that accepts and values people as they are. This is the Spirit that dwells within and beyond all Humanity. Throughout this book I use various words and phrases to try to describe the experience of the 'More

2

Than', emphasizing the fact that 'God' is real but not of the 'Old Man above the Sky' interpretation.

I have discovered something of this Perfect Love that I name as 'God' through the pilgrimages of faith of members of other religious groups. This God is the Indwelling Spirit summed up, in my experience, in the Hindi word 'Namaskarum' to mean 'the God in me welcoming and respecting the God in you.' I discovered this for myself while on an Air India flight from London to Mumbai. This God is accessed by and knowable to the Jew as 'Yahweh', to the Muslim as 'Allah', and to the Hindu in the different manifestations of the One God, and so on. But as a Christian, the Perfect Love that I experience and name as 'God' is made known to me in Jesus of Nazareth. I know that it is as I experience Jesus I also experience God and that is why it is Jesus whom I follow in my pilgrimage of faith.

I constantly try to look afresh at the God revealed throughout the Hebrew and Christian Testaments, but this God of my experience is no longer the God of anger, or vengeance, or blood, as made known to us through Hebrew prophets, historians, lawyers, poets and other religious leaders colored by their own often violent and oppressive history. Also, although it has to be as if looking through a darkened glass, I attempt to consider the Christian Testament through the eyes of the early Jewish Christian writers, as they struggled with the false oppressive gods of corrupted Temple leadership, and of the Roman Empire. All this is set within the context of their new revelation of the God in Jesus of Nazareth.

I want the Bible to live as it has never lived before. No matter how much I have known and experienced God in Jesus up to now, there is so much more to know and experience in the days to come.

The theology in this book is mine only in the sense that I subscribe whole-heartedly to it. But the theology is that of the scholarship of members of the Jesus Seminar and like-minded groupings. The only part that is mine is the exploration around the theology and its application to the post-modern world in which we now find ourselves. Over the last fifteen years of my spiritual pilgrimage, from an evangelical, charismatic theology and experience to where I am now, I have noted what others have said or written but not always accurately recorded the source. This is because, when I started jotting down new thoughts as I read or listened to others, I had no intention of writing a book. Although I have included a detailed list of books that have been the basis for my developing theology, this in no way makes up for failing to quote actual sources; but I am sure that all that I think is contained in the source material listed. I ask forgiveness of those writers whose works may have, albeit unintentionally, been plagiarized.

I take this opportunity to thank various people who have encouraged and challenged me in the writing of this book.

I am especially grateful to the people at the Methodist Church in Ludwick Way, Welwyn Garden City, 20 miles north of London, who accompanied me over five years of a shared pilgrimage of faith. Rev. Betty Saunders has been both an inspiration and a great encourager. John Bedigan has made critical, encouraging and always useful comments while I have been putting this book together. I also thank those of other congregations who have also supported and encouraged, and I hope been encouraged also, by our discussions together. It is also appropriate to thank those who have challenged me so much but who have perceived me as undermining the Christian faith and their own security zones. The challenges and refusals to allow me to preach in particular places always hurt, and, for example, to be told that I cannot be a Christian because I do not believe in the literalism of the Virgin Birth is particularly hurtful but understandable. Such challenges have always sent me back to think through again the spiritual journey that I am on. These challengers have ultimately served to confirm the rightness of a journey that is, by its very nature, provisional and in which – to paraphrase one of the eight points of the Progressive Christianity Network – the questions are more important than the answers, the journey more important than the arrival.

My thanks also go to Hugh Dawes and the other leaders of the Progressive Christianity Network – Britain, and to my spiritual guides, who to some will be considered 'double jeopardy' but to me are the 'New Female Trinity' of Karen Armstrong, Karen L. King and Elaine Pagels, and the 'New Male Trinity' of Marcus Borg, John Dominic Crossan and John Shelby Spong, without whom none of my spiritual journey would have been possible. I also acknowledge the help, friendship and encouragement that I have received from Rev. Ian Lawton and the people associated with Christ Community Church, Spring Lake, Michigan. To Di and the family, thanks for the encouragement and understanding as you have witnessed my spiritual journey from evangelical certainty to the excitement and joy of pilgrimage into the provisional and unknown, whatever and wherever that may be!

Blessings
John Churcher
[*Permission to Speak* Ministries]

Introduction

The wheel seems to have come full circle. At the age of eleven, and based upon my naïve political awareness and ignorance of the Church [even at that age Karl Marx meant more to me than Jesus of Nazareth, and my only visits to church having been for the annual primary school carol services], I destroyed my Gideon New Testament. I clearly remember taking a pen and writing across page after page 'opiate of the people'. And now, fifty years later, I seem to be 'destroying' the traditional theologies of the Church, but this time from an insider perspective. I can fully understand why many ministers leave the Christian Church, either having become Christian agnostics or even atheists as they find that the well of traditional theology is drying up in this post-Enlightenment, post-evangelical, post-Christian and perhaps even post-atheist society that so much of the 'first world' and 'new world' seem to be living in.

But this time I do not wish to destroy, but to find a new way to present and to live Jesus of Nazareth in this contemporary world. If we cannot find a new way to experience Jesus then I fear for the future of the Christian Church. We are at the crossroads. Either we continue down this dry, dusty and increasingly barren road into the desert from which there is no return, or we find the substance for the New Reformation from the visionary Bishop John A.T. Robinson in the 1960s and carried forward today by Bishop John Shelby Spong and other Jesus Seminar scholars. Theism may be dying but spirituality beyond religion experienced in the Unconditional, Perfect Love that is God is alive and well and eternal.

It is important to explain from where my thinking is coming, and if there is a shock from what follows on the pages of this book, let the shock be now rather than later!

6

To summarize my theology:

God is not the 'old Man above the sky', the Universal Master Chess Player, moving the pieces around to bless one and to condemn another. From pastoral experience this is where people can make so much pain for themselves in seeing God as the all-powerful manipulator of human life. The 'Why did God let this happen to me?' questions are thus often the first questions to be asked. I agree with Jack Spong that what we need is a new Christian Reformation in which God is no longer the 'old Man above the sky' who arbitrarily determines the fate of each one of us, but one in which God is the Indwelling Divine Spirit who accompanies us on our journey of faith, come what may, not protecting us from evil but sharing with us in all that happens, the good, the bad and the ugly.

Each faith community worships the same Divine Spirit but we each have our own cultural and linguistic gateways into the awareness of the God within. As a Christian I find my gateway into the awareness of the indwelling Divine Spirit in the uniqueness of Jesus of Nazareth. In Jesus I see all that God's Kingdom values and presence is about, but the Hindu, the Jew, the Muslim, the Sikh etc. have their own gateways into the awareness of the same Indwelling Divine Spirit.

The world was not created perfect and humanity did not fall from the Genesis Garden of Eden. These are sacred stories written within the restrictions of language, science, culture, etc. at the time of the Hebrew exile in Babylon some 600 years before Jesus. In my opinion we live in a continuous creation in which there is no conflict between post-Enlightenment science, astronomy, psychology, sociology, etc. and faith. Reading Teilhard de Chardin convinced me that Darwinism is just as applicable to human nature and spirituality as it is to the human physical and psychological state. Life has probably developed from the Big Bang and all, including we humans, are still developing. As part of the continuity of creation the Sacredness of Life itself invites us to live by the values of the Kingdom of God and to protect this world. Sadly we can just as easily reject the invitation of this Sacredness to cooperate in the process of continuous creation. This accounts, at least for me, as to why so much ill health is actually brought upon ourselves by our choice of life styles. Therefore, as I understand it, there is no Fall of Humanity, it is simply that we are not yet full of Humanity as was Jesus and we have a tendency too often to destroy more than we build.

As a Christian minister I spend much of my time dealing with issues of life and death. Illness, death and loss are not the result of an arbitrary God apparently blessing some and cruelly condemning others. Illness, death and loss are the results of humanity still developing and not yet being complete. Far from causing death and suffering the Indwelling Spirit within every person, regardless of creed or religion or faith experience, shares with us in our joys and sufferings. It is the Perfect Love that is God that encourages us and supports us – through family, friends and others when things are good or not so good [which is an excellent reason for being active within a church or faith community]. Whenever we experience the love and support of other people, what we are really experiencing is the love and support of the Indwelling Divine Spirit, through them. When we offer love, support and hospitality etc. to others, it is really we who are acting as the conduit of the Love that is God for others and for us.

The all-powerful God that we have been taught about for 2 millennia really is not the God I know. The Indwelling Divine Spirit is impotent and powerless unless we become the metaphorical hands, feet, eyes and ears of God, doing the work of Kingdom living in individuals and the community, protecting and completing the Creation. As such, and to quote Donald Rumsfeld, 'Stuff happens.' Life is life, and death is a natural part of life. God is with us in and through the experience. But, again from pastoral and personal experience, the inexplicable ['miracles'] happen from time to time. There is a spiritual world beyond our comprehension. But when confronted with someone who is seriously ill, I do not pray for a miracle of healing as much as I pray that doctors and nurses will use their utmost skills in protecting life, and that the person concerned will have the heart, the will, the courage and the strength to withstand the surgery etc., and to fight on until fighting is no longer possible. The strength to fight on can be greatly enhanced by the loving support and courage of those who are sharing in the pain and the uncertainty. The skills, the love and the courage, are all aspects of the Indwelling Spirit working through us humans as we love and care and give courage to those for whom courage seeps away under the pressures of ill-health and medical and surgical intervention. Even the skills of the doctors are the result of their living in the Indwelling Spirit, as they serve humanity.

Life is precious and we do what we can to preserve it as long as possible. But we make the choices and then live with the consequences. We do not usually have a choice as to how death should happen, but we do have a choice as to how the survivors survive and live again. To criticize God for death is to point the finger in the wrong direction. It simply indicates that we have believed the teaching of institutional Christian religion that God is an all-powerful, all-knowing God above the sky, who blesses those who do certain things and believe certain creeds, and condemns others who do not do or believe those things. Kingdom life is more than reciting creeds or praying a formulaic prayer of confession and conversion.

I am challenged by Borg's argument to be a 'panentheist' in that he sees all life in God and God in all life. Even where people reject the idea of God, still the Divine Spirit indwells them, it is just that they are unaware of the Presence.

With the exception of the writings of Luke, the Gospels and letters of the Christian Testament were primarily written by Jews for Jews from within the Jewish culture, language, and belief systems of the first century C.E. But the Jewish writers, readers and listeners interpreted Jesus through their Hebrew eyes and Hebrew Scriptures, and the original intentions of Paul, Peter, Mark, Matthew and John were very different to the concepts of Jesus developed down the later centuries by Gentiles using Jewish Scriptures to interpret the life and death of Jesus. Perhaps we have not fully grasped the significance that the second century leadership of the Christian communities was primarily Gentile, and that these later leaders unnecessarily literalized the Jewish interpretations of the life of Jesus of Nazareth.

The future of Christianity will depend upon the Followers of the Way of Jesus living Kingdom values rather than the Church highlighting, as the essential element for belonging, the need for assent to a set of standard creedal beliefs. Also, in this context, the Bible needs to be understood and interpreted as a human construct, that came out of the human struggle to understand what God was doing in the lives and within the history and experience of each writer. It is that spiritual struggle that turned the human understanding into sacred text. In a similar way, the Hebrew and Christian Scriptures remain words on the page until we, too, struggle with the same Divine Spirit to interpret what God is up to today. It is in this personal struggle to understand and discern that the Bible becomes Sacred for us. On that first Easter Sunday morning the Gospel stories tell us that Mary Magdalene went to the disciples with the news: "I have seen the Lord!" The message was that the One who was dead is alive! That was the experience of the Followers of Jesus in the years after that first Easter.

Our Gospel accounts of the death and resurrection of Jesus were all human attempts to describe the indescribable – that Jesus who was dead and buried was still very much alive in their daily experiences. As the first century moved to its close, the experiences of the early Followers of Jesus took place in times of continuing brutality and persecution under Roman occupation, and times of religious persecution and exclusion from their local synagogues. The writers of the Christian Testament were coming to their experiences and stories of Jesus – his life and death and that very real sense of the on-going presence with them – from within a culture in which things need not have been literally true or historically true for them to have been experienced as the truth. To understand the Easter stories we need to get our heads around that very difficult concept – things do not have to be actually true to be experientially true in the lives of the Followers of Jesus. For the early Christians, even though he was dead, Jesus continued to be experienced as alive, walking alongside them in their daily lives.

What I write now is not meant to appear to be condescending or belittling the Christian experiences and beliefs of others who think differently to me. If you believe that Jesus was physically raised from the dead on that Easter morning, then that is the Truth for you and I bless you in your pilgrimage and experience of faith. You are not wrong in your experiences of Jesus.

However, there are others who are equally Followers of the Way of Jesus for whom an empty tomb and a physically resurrected body are not important. What is important to all Followers of the Way of Jesus, regardless of the way we interpret and experience the Easter Sunday stories, is to be found in the words ascribed to Mary Magdalene, "I have seen the Lord!"

There is what is considered to be the conventional or the traditional Christianity of the institutional Church that attaches high importance to belief summed up in the words of ancient creeds and doctrines, but worked out in actions of love and service. Also, there is a radical and progressive understanding that depends, not upon statements of belief but upon values that underpin daily life and experience. Both approaches, the belief and the values, are based firmly upon interpretations and experiences of Jesus, and both are valid in the life of the Followers of the Way of Jesus.

For those who follow the traditional path, to be a Christian entails assent to certain statements of belief, such as the following taken from the Evangelical Alliance that represent 1.2 million Christians in the UK.

We believe in:

1. The one true God who lives eternally in three persons—the Father, the Son and the Holy Spirit.
2. The love, grace and sovereignty of God in creating, sustaining, ruling, redeeming and judging the world.
3. The divine inspiration and supreme authority of the Old and New Testament Scriptures, which are the written Word of God—fully trustworthy for faith and conduct.
4. The dignity of all people, made male and female in God's image, to love, be holy and care for creation, yet corrupted by sin, which incurs divine wrath and judgement.
5. The incarnation of God's eternal Son, the Lord Jesus Christ—born of the Virgin Mary; truly divine and truly human, yet without sin.
6. The atoning sacrifice of Christ on the cross: dying in our place, paying the price of sin and defeating evil, so reconciling us with God.
7. The bodily resurrection of Christ, the first fruits of our resurrection; his ascension to the Father, and his reign and mediation as the only Savior of the world.
8. The justification of sinners solely by the grace of God through faith in Christ.
9. The ministry of God the Holy Spirit, who leads us to repentance, unites us with Christ through new birth, empowers our discipleship and enables our witness.
10. The Church, the body of Christ both local and universal, the priesthood of all believers—given life by the Spirit and endowed with the Spirit's gifts to worship God and proclaim

the gospel, promoting justice and love.

11. The personal and visible return of Jesus Christ to fulfill the purposes of God, who will raise all people to judgement, bring eternal life to the redeemed and eternal condemnation to the lost, and establish a new heaven and new earth.

This is a more conventional form of Christianity but this understanding of being a Christian is, in my opinion, too much about a set of statements that give a structure to belief – but a structure that when interpreted to the letter of the law can be both rigid and judgmental towards those who do not agree with the eleven statements. It often condemns women to be second-class citizens in the ministry of some churches. It often condemns co-habiting heterosexual relationships that have not been blessed either within a religious community or in the registry office. It always seems to condemn those who enter single sex relationships.

But if these statements sum up your experience of Jesus and your walk of faith as a Christian, then you are *not* wrong in your experiences of Jesus, but I plead with you to let Perfect, Unconditional and Sacrificial Love be your Guide as you interpret the Scriptures and the eleven Evangelical Alliance points.

However, to those who experience Jesus day by day, not in a statement of beliefs but in a set of values, I offer the following, not as a creed but as guidance. These are adapted by the Progressive Christianity Network – Britain, from those 8 points of the original the Progressive Christian Network, The Center for Progressive Christianity in USA.

We are Christians who:

1. Have found an approach to God through the life and teachings of Jesus.
2. Recognize the faithfulness of other people who have other names for the gateway to God's realm, and acknowledge that

their ways are true for them, as our ways are true for us.

3. Understand the sharing of bread and wine in Jesus' name to be a representation of an ancient vision of God's feast for all peoples.

4. Invite all people to participate in our community and worship life without insisting that they become like us in order to be acceptable (including but not limited to):
   - believers and agnostics
   - conventional Christians and questioning skeptics
   - women and men
   - those of all sexual orientations and gender identities
   - those of all races and cultures
   - those of all classes and abilities
   - those who hope for a better world and those who have lost hope.

5. Know that the way we behave toward one another and toward other people is the fullest expression of what we believe;

6. Find more grace in the search for understanding than we do in dogmatic certainty, more value in questioning than in absolutes.

7. Form ourselves into communities dedicated to equipping one another for the work we feel called to do: striving for peace and justice among all people; protecting and restoring the integrity of all God's creation; and bringing hope to those Jesus called the least of his sisters and brothers.

8. Recognize that being followers of Jesus is costly, and entails selfless love, conscientious resistance to evil, and renunciation of privilege.

This is something like a continuum, with the Progressive Christianity Network to the left and the Evangelical Alliance to the right. I guess that many Christians today will not be at either end of this continuum but will be comfortable somewhere between the two. What is important however to all Followers of the Way of Jesus, regardless of the way we interpret and experience the Easter Sunday stories, is still to be found in the words ascribed to Mary Magdalene, "I have seen the Lord!"

To summarize my understanding and experience of Jesus of Nazareth.

Jesus was the breaker of all barriers that separate, and the final barrier to be broken was that between life and death. That was the experience of the early Christian writers and that should be our experience today. The story of the empty tomb will be for many Christians an historical fact that is unchallengeable. But for others the story of the empty tomb symbolizes the truth and the reality that nothing can nor should separate us from the Sacred coming to us in one another every moment of every day.

The Easter story is not simply something to be remembered and celebrated annually but it is a truth to be experienced every moment of every day. Good Friday and Easter Sunday are not just stories and traditions from the past – they are to be our daily experiences. Ours is a Calvary experience every time we put the needs of others before those of ourselves. The Empty Tomb and the Easter Sunday Resurrection experience is not something for which we wait beyond death, but it is ours to be experienced everyday in the here and now. As we die to self-interest so we are raised again to new life. Every little death to self-interest and superficiality is followed by a resurrection experience that makes us a little more like Jesus; it makes us a little more Human and therefore a little more Divine.

When I take the bread and wine in Holy Communion, I interpret these as symbols of taking the Unconditional, Sacrificial and Perfect Love shown to us in Jesus so that the more I allow this Love to be my way of life then it is I and not the Church, who becomes the risen 'Body of Christ.' In this way, the Body of Christ is not an institutional body but it is Christians who become the

Living Body.

Having said all that, my prayer is that I do not just experience Jesus as found in the words ascribed to Mary Magdalene, "I have seen the Lord!" but that I will daily experience Jesus in all whom I meet – in those I enjoy being with and in those I would rather cross over the road to avoid. Of course, to meet Jesus is not a 'cross the road' experience – it is to be found in the words of Matthew's Gospel chapter 25.

For I was hungry and you gave me something to eat, I was thirsty and you gave me something to drink, I was a stranger and you invited me in, I needed clothes and you clothed me, I was sick and you looked after me, I was in prison and you came to visit me. Then the righteous will answer him, 'Lord, when did we see you hungry and feed you, or thirsty and give you something to drink? When did we see you a stranger and invite you in, or needing clothes and clothe you? When did we see you sick or in prison and go to visit you?' The King will reply, 'I tell you the truth, whatever you did for one of the least of these, you did for me.'

The Empty Tomb, whatever that was, is not just something from the past but it is to be lived and experienced today and every day. No matter whether you believe that Jesus was physically raised from the dead or spiritually raised from the dead, the important point is that we can all give daily enthusiastic approval to the joyful Easter shout of praise: "The Lord is here! His Spirit is with us!"

Chapter One

In The Beginning

There are only two historical facts concerning Jesus of which I am certain, and that can be verified from independent sources. The first, according to Josephus, is that there was a Jesus [of Nazareth?] who was crucified by the Roman occupation force and yet his followers some six decades later were claiming that he continued to live in their life experiences. The second obvious fact is that because Jesus is recorded as having been executed then he must have been born.

Now the evidence becomes more circumstantial as I consider the continuing claims of his impact upon his followers. There must have been something out of the ordinary about the life of Jesus, his wisdom teaching and actions, some of which would have been history remembered, history interpreted and history developed into theology. Such progress in thinking would have included non-historical human explanations, making Jesus of Nazareth into the New Moses and others of the ancient Hebrew Prophets. I am convinced by Borg's argument that the Christian Testament, like the Hebrew Testament before it, was predominantly allegory, metaphor and Midrash [the taking of ancient stories and reworking them into the contemporary times of the later writers] and not accurate history committed to memory.

It is important that some thought is given as to how the Hebrew and Christian Testaments are interpreted today. As an example I refer to an interesting and sometimes disturbing book entitled *The Pagan Christ* by Tom Harpur. Although he is onto something very important concerning Jesus of Nazareth and the God Within, I find it difficult to agree with him when he talks of what appears to me to be little more than linguistic slight of hand. For example, he links the ancient Bethan to Bethanu from whence we arrive at Bethany; Meri to Mary and then to Martha. But Harpur, and those scholars upon whom he bases his whole thesis, offer a very persuasive argument that both the Hebrew and Christian Testaments simply are retelling the ancient Egyptian, Pagan stories of the Spirit of God Within, applied to both Moses and Jesus. In these ancient Sun Worshipper stories, God became human to suffer, die and to be resurrected to New Life. According to Harpur, these ancient stories were never intended to be literalized or personified into the person of Jesus of Nazareth but they remain what they have always been, eternal metaphors of the life cycle.

Harpur in North America, along with many others including Jonathan Bartley in the UK, argues that it was the Early Church Fathers and the impact of the conversion of Emperor Constantine and subsequent Creedal declarations of the 4th century that set in stone a literalized and personified masculine God in the God/Man Jesus of Nazareth. Harpur further argues that to cover up their woeful plagiarism of the ancient Pagan Spirit stories, these 4th century Church Fathers then went on to destroy people, books and whole libraries, so that the alternative literature from, for example, the Gnostics would be lost forever. And for 1600 years the vandalism of the Church Fathers was covered up, but then came the 19th century discovery at Oxhyrenchus, and the mid-20th century discoveries at Nag Hammadi and the caves above the Dead Sea. Whether or not Harpur's understanding of early Church history is accurate or just jaundiced, is a debate for another occasion.

However, according to Harpur et al., the myths of the Ancient Pagan stories tell us that, as we realize the Truth of the God Within, so we are experiencing the constant process of dying to self and of being raised to new life. And what is more Christian than that? As I ponder the arguments put forward by Harpur, I reject his thesis that 'Jesus' was merely a linguistic creation and not an historical figure. However, Harpur leads me to ask at least two questions: the first, "Did Jesus of Nazareth intentionally model himself on the well-known but ancient Egyptian myths of the God Within?" and the second question concerns the Christian Testament writers: "Did Paul, Mark, Matthew, Luke, Peter, John, etc., intentionally interpret the ancient Egyptian myths and apply them to the human Jesus?"

Whatever, we are now in a new world of discovery available to all, and not just to the scholars, the clergy and the seminaries. We have access to additional source information about both the historical Jesus and the early Churches. Now it is legitimate to read afresh the Hebrew and Christian Testaments as intended by the writers, as analogy, metaphor, Midrash and mythology. But because the stories of the Hebrew and Christian Testaments no longer need to be interpreted, either literally or necessarily as historically true, this is not to say that the Bible as a whole has nothing to say to us in the 21st century. When mythology is read as mythology and metaphor as metaphor and allegory as allegory, or as Karen Armstrong's 'logos' and 'mythos', then a new depth of Spiritual awareness and understanding of the human condition can come sweeping through.

Evangelical Christians often proclaim that there is a 'God-shaped void in the heart of every human' and that only Jesus can fill this void. Surely there can be nothing further from the truth? Within each and every person, regardless of creed or religious experience, there is the Presence [not the void] of the Sacred. Even though this Presence of Perfect and Compassionate Love may not be recognized, it is the true spiritual Incarnation. It happened to Jesus, and it has happened to you and to me. All the power of Perfect Love is incarnated within all people, for all are temples of the Spirit that is God. In my opinion, what was so special about Jesus was his living awareness of the Sacred Spirit within him. This enabled him to respond in such an open way that he knew and experienced the fullness of what it meant to be human. It was through this that those who were close to him knew that they were in the presence of the Sacred.

That same Incarnate Power of Perfect Love is within you and me so that we can respond and grow towards the revelation and experience that people witnessed in Jesus of Nazareth. Far from there being a God-shaped void within us, we have the sleeping giant of Perfect Unconditional Love waiting to be recognized, responded to and lived by us all. With such recognition comes personal responsibility not to 'off load' our sins and sense of guilt onto the Jesus created and maintained by the Church, but to respond by rejecting our personal and corporate selfishness and, instead, practicing the Perfect Love within.

This is the Power that will transform humanity and the whole of Creation. But the empty, hollow literalist and fundamentalist interpretations of the Jesus of the Gospels and the creeds of the 3rd and 4th centuries will not bring about such desperately needed transformation. Indeed, while there exist literalists and fundamentalists in any religion there will always be exclusivism and division. However, it is by the recognition and willing acceptance of the Incarnation of the Spirit of Perfect Love Within all people that will bring an age of respect and peace for and between all.

Just before I left theological college a tutor said, to me, "Do you have the arrogance to say that the Christian Church has got it wrong for 1600 years?" I wish that I had had the courage at the time to say, "Well, yes, I am saying that. But this is no more arrogant than the Christian Church continuing to maintain a theology that is based upon [a] both the dubious impact of Constantine and the 4th century Creeds that resulted in the excommunication and destruction of detractors and their writings [some kind of Stalinist revisionism by the victorious wing of the Early Church Fathers?] and [b] the leading astray of the Followers of the Way of Jesus, from their precarious but personally powerful position as 'ginger' groups on the edge of society and into becoming power brokers at the centre of Empire". I am convinced that the impact of Constantine and the Council at Nicea prostituted the real open, barrier breaking and unconditional message of Jesus of Nazareth for the sake of political power and influence.

Theophilus and the background to Luke's Gospel

So we turn to Luke's Gospel. This is not a work of fiction, but it is a heavily edited biography of Jesus based upon second-hand information. As such, Luke's Gospel cannot and must not be read as a factually correct record of all that Jesus said and did. It cannot and must not be read as literal truth. But to understand Luke's style of writing we have to go back to the opening verses in this Gospel.

> Many people have tried to tell the story of what God has done amongst us. They wrote what we had been told by the ones who were there in the beginning and saw what happened. So I made a careful study of everything and then decided to write to tell you exactly what took place. Honorable Theophilus, I have done this to let you know the truth about what you have heard.

To ignore the scholarship surrounding, for example, who was the Theophilus to whom Luke was writing, will mean that we cannot understand either the Gospel's intent or its content. I am convinced by the scholarship that dates the writing of Luke's Gospel to the late 80s or early 90s C.E. Therefore it is important to note several things from these opening four verses of Luke's Gospel.

1] Luke was not amongst the original disciples of Jesus and probably had never met Jesus in person; all that is in this Gospel is the result of Luke probably studying available sources such as the letters of Paul and Peter, the Q source, and the Gospels of Thomas, Mark and Matthew, all reflecting the stories of those who had been with Jesus.

2] Who was it at the beginning of the ministry of Jesus who would have passed on these eye witness stories? It could have been Simon Peter and his brother Andrew, and James and John, the sons of Zebedee, all commercial fishermen; or perhaps it was Philip; or Nathaniel who was also known as Bartholomew; or Matthew, the tax collector; or even Thomas the Doubter, who was probably the most honest of all the disciples and the writer of possibly the earliest Gospel that we have, although it is not included in the canon of scripture; or James the son of Alpheus; or Simon the Zealot who was probably the political activist in the original group; or Judas the son of James [this was not the Judas who betrayed Jesus]. But we must not forget that other people were with Jesus almost from the beginning who may also have influenced Luke's writings – for example, Mary Magdalene, Joanna and Susanna.

3] Luke never wrote this as a Gospel of verbatim accuracy [none of the four Gospels in the Christian Testament were historically accurate] but its uniqueness was in stating that he was combining and editing other stories and works into a biography of Jesus. In those opening four verses, Luke assured his readers that both his ordering of the stories and the words used were carefully chosen by him.

4] Luke never wrote this Gospel for hundreds of generations and millions of people to read but he actually wrote it to one person, Theophilus, to help him understand what he had been told by others. In the Coptic Christian understanding, this Theophilus is thought to have been a Jew living in Alexandria. However, in Greek, the word 'Theophilus' means 'Friend of God' and so

Luke's Gospel and his second volume, the Book of Acts, may have been written for any who considered themselves to be a 'Friend of God.'

Another tradition is that Theophilus was an important Prefect of Rome, possibly the brother of Emperor Vespasian, converted perhaps by Paul. Yet another tradition suggests that Theophilus was Paul's lawyer in Rome and Luke wrote the Gospel and Book of Acts to give the lawyer sufficient background to help him defend Paul in Court. If this is the case, then the Gospel and the Book of Acts would have been written in the early 60s C.E., going against the common scholarly position that both the Gospel of Luke and the Book of Acts were written in the late 80s or early 90s.

However, there is a further theory that I find the most compelling, that the intended recipient of the Gospel was Theophilus bar Ananas, a Sadducee and member of the wealthy High Priest family. He was the High Priest in the Jerusalem Temple from 37 to 41 C.E. during the latter years of the reign of Herod Antipas and immediately before Antipas was replaced by order of the Emperor Caligula – that is if one accepts the historical accuracy of Josephus's book *Antiquities of the Jews* written in 93 or 94 C.E. I repeat that this was also the time when most scholars place Luke writing his Gospel and the Book of Acts, and just before the time when John's Gospel was written.

If this is the intended recipient then this could explain why Luke's Gospel begins with the words 'Honorable Theophilus' indicating someone of immense importance. The use of the word 'honorable' would indicate either the Roman Governor or the High Priest, and there was no Roman Governor of that name but there was a High Priest called Theophilus! If the dating of Luke's Gospel is accurately placed in the 9th decade C.E. then this Theophilus would have been an elderly man trying to make sense of the previous 60 years. Perhaps Theophilus had requested Luke to write this Gospel for his own spiritual journey to make sense of Judaism beyond the destruction of the Temple and the end of the Sadducees as an influential leadership party? In my opinion, as I struggle to understand the person and work of Jesus, this is a most profound statement: Luke took this opportunity to help Theophilus in his struggle to understand Jesus, not as being in opposition to Judaism but as a reformer of Judaism.

Notice also the lack of accusation against Caiaphas by name and his role in the trial and execution of Jesus – the references in Luke chapter 22 are to the 'high priest.' This is especially so as Theophilus bar Ananas was the brother in law of Joseph Caiaphas who was the High Priest before whom Jesus was brought after Judas had betrayed him.

Also of significance in support of my assertion that the intended recipient of this Gospel was Theophilus bar Ananas and the purpose was 're-education', is that Luke highlighted the physical resurrection of Jesus in opposition to the Sadducees who had rejected such a possibility.

Apart from the story of the birth of Jesus, no other Gospel has the contents of the opening two chapters of Luke's Gospel. By starting his Gospel as he did, Luke, the Gentile convert and writing for a predominantly Gentile audience, placed Jesus firmly within Judaism.

Background to the birth stories of Jesus

Countless people have said to me over recent years, in Britain, North America and in Eastern Europe that the whole Christian message is suspect owing to the biologically unbelievable Virgin Birth of Jesus. They also often reject choirs of angels and the wise men, and so on. But I have attempted to explain to them that I find it far more deepening for my faith to see the contexts of the writings of the two different Gospel accounts of the Birth of Jesus [Matthew and Luke] as 'stories of encouragement' rather than literal biographic accuracy.

The symbolism and political context of the birth stories are so much more relevant for me today in our broken world than interpreting these Matthew or Luke stories as being historically accurate. I know, from 30 years active involvement and leadership within the evangelical and charismatic tradition, the importance of the Virgin Birth and the inerrancy of Scripture. However, I am now what is often referred to as a 'post evangelical' and unlike many of these, I have not walked away from the Church but I have found a deeper more relevant faith in the man, Jesus of Nazareth, who was made into the Christ of the Church.

Setting aside the commercialism that surrounds Christmas in this age – the Christmas decorations and the television advertisements that seem to begin in mid-autumn; the flashing street-lights and the Father Christmases in shops; the fact that December the 25th is not the actual day on which Jesus was born, and that Christmas coincides with an ancient pre-Christian ceremony that celebrated the mid-winter solstice when the light begins to conquer the darkness of winter – setting aside these things, Christmas really is a wonderful time because into the darkness of the life of the world we find the Christian hope of Jesus of Nazareth who can be seen as a Light of the Sacred penetrating the evolutionary darkness in which humankind lives. It was over a period of several Christmases that brought me the gifts of books that re-shaped my understanding of the birth stories of Jesus. These included Spong's *Born of A Woman*, and *Rescuing the Bible from Fundamentalism*, and Borg's *Meeting Jesus Again for the First Time*.

And as I read these books I became increasingly aware that, in the lead up to Christmas, Isaiah 9 is often quoted [erroneously] as a foretelling of the birth of Jesus. In the section that is often entitled 'To Us a Child Is Born' we read:

1 Nevertheless, there will be no more gloom for those who

were in distress. In the past he humbled the land of Zebulun and the land of Naphtali, but in the future he will honor Galilee of the Gentiles, by the way of the sea, along the Jordan. 2 The people walking in darkness have seen a great light; on those living in the land of the shadow of death a light has dawned. 3 You have enlarged the nation and increased their joy; they rejoice before you as people rejoice at the harvest, as men rejoice when dividing the plunder. 4 For as in the day of Midian's defeat, you have shattered the yoke that burdens them, the bar across their shoulders, the rod of their oppressor. 5 Every warrior's boot used in battle and every garment rolled in blood will be destined for burning, will be fuel for the fire. 6 For to us a child is born, to us a son is given, and the government will be on his shoulders. And he will be called Wonderful Counselor, Mighty God, Everlasting Father, Prince of Peace. 7 Of the increase of his government and peace there will be no end. He will reign on David's throne and over his kingdom, establishing and upholding it with justice and righteousness from that time on and forever. The zeal of the LORD Almighty will accomplish this."

But Isaiah was not prophesying the birth of Jesus but was referring to the birth of Hezekiah. Joseph Jensen and William H. Irwin writing in *The New Jerome Biblical Commentary* [1993; p 236], relate this First Isaiah passage to the Holy War Tradition that all victories in battle come from the hand of Yahweh God and that the new King would not need the help of advisors or spin-doctors. Earlier dependence upon such as these was seen by Isaiah to have led to the downfall of Ahaz. It was much later that this Isaiah passage came to be applied by the Gospel writers to Jesus. But nevertheless, in my experience of Jesus of Nazareth, most of Isaiah's foretelling of Hezekiah's birth contains Eternal Truth and applies to both Jesus and to us. We are the people who walk in darkness but have seen a great light. We are those who live in a land of the shadow [of death?] but have seen a light shone because to us a child is born and the names that are given ring true in our experience: wonderful Counselor, mighty God, eternal Father, Prince of Peace. This is a brilliant application of Gospel hindsight!

But there are other parallels between the Gospel of Luke and the much earlier stories contained in the Hebrew Testament, and especially in the Torah (those opening five books of our Bible that were and are still read today in their entirety over the course of each synagogue year), along with the theme of 'Immanuel – God with us.'

The earliest Followers of the Way of Jesus were Jews who continued to worship in the synagogues, alongside those Jews who rejected the message and witness of Jesus; and it is within the context of the synagogue that our contemporary Biblical scholarship from such as Michael Goulder and Jack Spong place the Gospel stories. Goulder suggests that the writer of Luke's Gospel was writing the stories to coincide, as far as possible, with the stories read each Sabbath day in the synagogue, stories from the Torah along with stories from other parts of the Hebrew Bible. Luke wrote parallel stories to acknowledge that 'the Jewish leaders of the past were great - but Jesus is greater.'

As has been the case over millennia, some people still read the Gospel stories as historically accurate biographies of the life of Jesus the Christ. However, others read them as human interpretations of the life of Jesus of Nazareth with little historical fact involved.

Whatever, after the dedication to Theophilus, Luke's account does not continue straight into the foretelling of the birth of Jesus but with the foretelling of the birth of John the Baptist. Immediately Luke's readers and listeners were reminded of important families from Hebrew antiquity.

Luke 1: 5 – 25
An angel tells about the birth of John the Baptist

5 In the time of Herod king of Judea there was a priest named Zechariah, who belonged to the priestly division of Abijah; his wife Elizabeth was also a descendant of Aaron. 6 Both of them were upright in the sight of God, observing all the Lord's commandments and regulations blamelessly. 7 But they had no children, because Elizabeth was barren; and they were both well along in years.

8 Once when Zechariah's division was on duty and he was serving as priest before God, 9 he was chosen by lot, according to the custom of the priesthood, to go into the temple of the Lord and burn incense. 10 And when the time for the burning of incense came, all the assembled worshipers were praying outside.

11 Then an angel of the Lord appeared to him, standing at the right side of the altar of incense. 12 When Zechariah saw him, he was startled and was gripped with fear. 13 But the angel said to him: "Do not be afraid, Zechariah; your prayer has been heard. Your wife Elizabeth will bear you a son, and you are to give him the name John. 14 He will be a joy and delight to you, and many will rejoice because of his birth, 15 for he will be great in the sight of the Lord. He is never to take wine or other fermented drink, and he will be filled with the Holy Spirit even from birth. 16 Many of the people of Israel will he bring back to the Lord their God. 17 And he will go on before the Lord, in the spirit and power of Elijah, to turn the hearts of the fathers to their children and the disobedient to the wisdom of the righteous—to make ready a people prepared for the Lord."

18 Zechariah asked the angel, "How can I be sure of this? I am an old man and my wife is well along in years."

19 The angel answered, "I am Gabriel. I stand in the

presence of God, and I have been sent to speak to you and to tell you this good news. 20 And now you will be silent and not able to speak until the day this happens, because you did not believe my words, which will come true at their proper time."

21 Meanwhile, the people were waiting for Zechariah and wondering why he stayed so long in the temple. 22 When he came out, he could not speak to them. They realized he had seen a vision in the temple, for he kept making signs to them but remained unable to speak. 23 When his time of service was completed, he returned home. 24 After this his wife Elizabeth became pregnant and for five months remained in seclusion. 25 "The Lord has done this for me," she said. "In these days he has shown his favor and taken away my disgrace among the people."

In reading and understanding the Bible it is always important to note the meaning of the names and the family connections - and verse 5 introduces us to the priest Zechariah from the family of Abijah, and to his wife Elizabeth descended from Aaron, the brother of Moses.

We know the importance of Aaron but who was Abijah? He can be found in I Kings 14 and II Chronicles 13. He was the King who reigned for 3 years following the death of his father Rehoboam. Neither father nor son were particularly faithful to Yahweh God, and they only called upon God when they were in times of danger. It seems as though Abijah talked the talk, rather then walked the walk. And while Abijah talked about the impending battle, Jeroboam and his army surrounded Abijah and would have had the eventual victory except that, according to the writer of the Book of Kings, Yahweh God had made the earlier promise to King David that his descendants would rule over the people of Yahweh God. And so, against the odds, Abijah was victorious even though he did not deserve the victory.

So it is important for Luke to trace back the lineage of John the Baptist to King David because it gave validity to John's supporting role to David's greater descendent, Jesus himself; and perhaps the link between Rehoboam and Abijah to John the Baptist demonstrated that Yahweh God's love and promises were such that even those who failed as followers of God were ultimately accepted and forgiven by God?

Jack Spong, in his book, *Born of a Woman,* invites us to look carefully at the structure of Luke's introduction to the elderly and childless couple, Zechariah and Elizabeth. Here, as Spong clearly states, we have a Biblical pattern repeated over and over again, the pattern of annunciation, that is the announcement of a special birth, followed by the naming of the child and finally the statement about the child's destiny. This is Jewish rabbinic Midrash at work: later writers taking stories of the past and reworking them to make sense of their present. Spong points out that it is there in:

- Genesis 16 concerning Ishmael;
- Genesis 17 concerning Isaac;
- 1 Kings 13 concerning Josiah;
- Isaiah 7 concerning Immanuel;
- 1 Chronicles 22 concerning Solomon;
- Luke 1:16-17 concerning John the Baptist;
- Luke 1:28-33 concerning Jesus.

Even though Luke was a Gentile by birth, he knew his Hebrew Scriptures and he placed Jesus in the line of the greats of the Jewish faith by adopting this annunciation, naming and destiny format of writing. But not only is Luke concerned with adding John the Baptist and Jesus to this format, but he also makes a further parallel with other older childless couples of the Hebrew Scriptures who go on to receive the gift of a son beyond the normal age for such an event.

Further examples include Abraham and Sarah in Genesis 16 and 18 concerning the birth of Isaac, and Elkanah and Hannah in 1 Samuel 1 and 2 concerning the birth of Samuel. Both Isaac and Samuel played major roles in the salvation history of the Jews, Isaac as a patriarch and Samuel as a prophet. But Luke draws even more parallels. Sarah in the Genesis story is barren and Elizabeth in the Gospel story is barren. Both encountered angels who foretold the birth of sons. Both Abraham in the Genesis story and Zechariah in the Gospel story refused to believe the message of the angels but both were assured that everything is possible with God.

There was Isaac and his wife Rebekah in Genesis 25. When they discovered that they were expecting twins, the same pattern was repeated – annunciation/announcement while the children were still in the womb, followed by the naming of the children and the setting of their destinies. And how did Rebekah become aware of the annunciation? By the leaping of the twins in her womb, so much so that Rebekah enquired of the Lord about them. It is written that God told Rebekah that the first son to be born was to be called Esau, meaning 'completion' as he would be born covered in body hair such as a man would be covered.

The other twin was to be named Jacob, meaning 'one who holds the heel' – in other words, the second of the twins to be born. However, the destiny is set as the older son, Esau, would one day be secondary to the younger son, Jacob. What is the Midrash parallel of Luke's account? John the Baptist was to be born before Jesus, and when Mary told Elizabeth about her pregnancy and the angel's message that the name of her unborn son was to be Jesus, the fetus of John the Baptist is said to have leapt in Elizabeth's womb. Although John the Baptist would be born first, he would eventually be secondary to his younger cousin Jesus. John the Baptist is Esau all over again – and Jesus is Jacob. But here I must add a 'health warning': I discussed the content of this section with the Chairman of a synagogue and he accepted all the points that I am making concerning the links between the Hebrew and Christian Testaments. However, he did point out that such links are not as simple as I suggest in that the parallel of John the Baptist and Esau does not sit well as Esau was a brute, a man of force and shallow spirituality who would, from a Jewish perspective, sell his birthright for a mess of pottage. John, by all accounts was a much more spiritual person.

But there are other Midrash parallels pointed out by Spong: first in Genesis 30 v 23, where Rachel, the jealous and barren but favorite wife of Jacob is said to have been remembered by God and promised a son. Such was the attitude towards infertility in those days that Rachel thought that her barrenness was a disgrace and a punishment from God. Her response to the news that she would give birth to Joseph was "God has taken away my disgrace". And what did Luke have Elizabeth say when she was told that she would no longer be barren? "God has taken away my disgrace and people will no longer look down upon me."

Jacob's other wife, Leah, in Genesis 29 v 30 proclaims that she will be called 'blessed' because she had children. Note that this is what Luke put into the mouth of Mary, mother of Jesus in the *Magnificat*, "From now on all people will say that God has blessed me".

Coincidence after coincidence after coincidence, or is Luke struggling some 80 - 90 years after the birth of Jesus to make sense of the Jesus experience? In that struggle with the Spirit of God, Luke is using Midrash to retell the stories of Jewish antiquity to put Jesus in the right place, Bethlehem, David's Town, at the right time and of the right lineage to really be the long prophesied and awaited Messiah.

In my understanding, Luke was not writing factual history when he wrote the stories of Elizabeth and Zechariah, or Elizabeth and Mary, or John and Jesus. But that does not mean that there is no truth in the explanatory fiction. The Followers of the Way of Jesus experienced such a depth of wisdom and sacrificial love in Jesus that led them to conclude that in meeting him they had met with God. And that is the truth for us today. It is in our giving and receiving of sacrificial love that we will meet Jesus, and often that will be in the most surprising people and often in the most surprising of places. The parallels are fiction but the Sacred Truth of Immanuel, 'God with us', is fact.

There are yet other parallels in the Gospel of Luke - this time concerning the birth of Jesus. Luke draws his inspiration and his parallel for the birth stories of Jesus from the ancient stories of Jacob. But, the health warning again, from the point of view of Followers of the Way of Jesus, we need to be aware of the limits to the parallel as Jacob was a cheat and Jesus was full of humanity through which people experienced divinity. In Genesis 32 we read of Jacob leaving his father-in-law, Laban, a relationship that was not the best. Cheating and a lack of trust marked much of Jacob's relationships, and finally Jacob departed with the intention of meeting again with his brother Esau, the brother whom Jacob had cheated out of his birthright a long while before.

It is written that God's angels visited Jacob *en route* after which Jacob, to ease the way ahead, sent peace offerings to Esau. However, the envoys returned to Jacob with the news that Esau, accompanied by 400 men was not far behind. Anxiety got the better of Jacob and he decided upon a two-stage strategy. The first was to send yet more peace offerings, and then when darkness fell, he escorted his wives and eleven children, and all his remaining belongings, across the river to a place of safety. When Jacob was content that all his remaining goods and property, including his family, were safe, he returned alone to await the arrival of Esau. Having crossed back, according to the story in Genesis 32, an unknown man attacked him and wrestled with Jacob for what remained of the night.

But, according to the story, this was no ordinary man but an angel of God. The struggle was long and hard fought, and the angel could only overcome Jacob by putting Jacob's hip out of joint. Jacob, a cheat and a thief, then realized that his opponent was no ordinary man and immediately asked for a blessing from God. As happened from time to time in the ancient stories, God responded by changing the names of people, thereby giving them new authority or roles. This time it was Jacob whom God renamed 'Israel', meaning 'Prince of God.' Jacob/Israel named that place of meeting with God 'Peniel', meaning the place where Jacob believed that he had met God face to face and lived.

The action then moves to Genesis 35 where we read of Jacob/Israel travelling back to his hometown with his pregnant wife Rachel. There are no prizes for guessing the name of the hometown to which Jacob/Israel was returning! Bethlehem, the town that later became the birthplace of David and subsequently claimed to be the birthplace of Jesus. It is there in Bethlehem that Rachel's baby was born and he was named 'Benjamin', meaning "Son of my right hand." To this day, to be "the right hand man" is to be the most important and the one to be trustworthy to do the father's behest. Here is another Midrash parallel: who, according to Luke 22 will sit at the right hand of God? None other than Jesus who called himself the Son of Man!

Consider other parallels. Jacob took his pregnant wife Rachel to Bethlehem and then some 1600 years later, Joseph took his pregnant wife Mary to Bethlehem. An angel of God met with Jacob and an angel of God met with Joseph to explain the situation, and an angel of God met with the shepherds to tell them of the birth of Jesus. These are intentional Midrashic parallels rather than mere coincidences.

Luke 1: 46 – 55
The Magnificat

46 And Mary said: "My soul glorifies the Lord   47 and my spirit rejoices in God my Savior, 48 for he has been mindful of

the humble state of his servant. From now on all generations will call me blessed, 49 for the Mighty One has done great things for me, holy is his name. 50 His mercy extends to those who fear him, from generation to generation. 51 He has performed mighty deeds with his arm; he has scattered those who are proud in their inmost thoughts. 52 He has brought down rulers from their thrones but has lifted up the humble. 53 He has filled the hungry with good things but has sent the rich away empty. 54 He has helped his servant Israel, remembering to be merciful 55 to Abraham and his descendants forever, even as he said to our fathers."

It is very important to acknowledge two points about the Magnificat. First, that this angelic visitation never really happened, because if it did then the other Gospel writers and the letters of Paul would surely have made reference to this song of praise from Mary; and, secondly, that this is not an original song written by Luke or even a song sung by Mary, mother of Jesus. The Magnificat is another example of Jewish Midrash, taking the words of the ancient Hebrew Scriptures and making them fresh and new in the life of Jesus and his followers. Luke has lifted this Song of Mary from 1 Samuel 2:1-10 where Hannah the mother of Samuel offers a prayer as she dedicates her young son to God.

In *Born of a Woman*, Spong again points out that both the 1 Samuel and the Luke 1 prayers emphasize that the all-powerful God of Hebrew literature had chosen these two women to be mothers of special sons, and the same God referred to in the Books of Samuel is the same God referred to by Luke. This is the God who would humble the rich and exalt and bless the poor.

But what else is Luke saying about Samuel and Jesus? Some 1100 years before Jesus, Samuel was both the last of the Judges to rule the Hebrews and the first of the foremost Hebrew prophets. As such, Samuel was the connection between the two eras that took the Hebrew people from the Period of Judges to the Period of the Kings. The first was King David, followed by his son Solomon. I am sure that Luke the Gentile, convert and outsider, was saying to his readers and listeners, "Look how Samuel connected the eras, and this is what Jesus of Nazareth is also doing. Jesus is connecting the Old Covenant with the Jews to the New Covenant with all people."

Luke has other parallels. The name 'Samuel' means 'a child from God', and in Luke chapter 1:30-32 Luke puts a similar message to Mary into the mouth of the Angel, "Don't be afraid! God is pleased with you and you will have a son. His name will be Jesus. He will be great and will be called the Son of the Most High God". In applying Midrash to the ancient stories, Luke presented his followers with what we have come to call 'the Magnificat'. Luke had recreated the story of Samuel, making the point to the Jews and Gentiles alike that no matter how great and important Samuel had been, Jesus was greater and more important.

Luke continues to draw the parallel between Samuel and Jesus. In the 1st Book of Samuel, Hannah, mother of Samuel, dedicated her son as a Nazarite. That word comes from the Hebrew 'nazir' which according to Numbers, chapter 6 v 8, means 'consecrated and set apart for God to use in a unique and special way.' But I wonder if it is a case of mistaken translation or mistaken transcription of the Scriptures when considering Jesus being a 'spiritual' Nazarite consecrated and set apart for God to use in a unique and special way, and one who came from Nazareth and therefore known as a Nazarene? Or perhaps Jesus was both, a spiritual nazir who happened to be born and to live and to begin his ministry in Nazareth?

Remember that we are reading and interpreting these stories and parables as we always do, from a western post-modern mindset that gives us a very different interpretation and under-standing to those Jewish and Gentile followers of the Way of Jesus at the time when the Gospels were written. In all probability, Luke's original Jewish listeners and readers would have known these significant nazir links that were being made between Samuel and Jesus.

Spong also invites us to think about further parallels between Samuel the nazir and Jesus. Luke's Jewish followers of the Way of Jesus would also have known that to become a 'nazir,' the Jewish man or woman would undergo an initiation rite that lasted for a minimum period of 30 days, during which time he or she would have to go without wine, not cut their hair and not touch a dead body. After this, the one who was determined to become a nazir would have to be ritually cleansed in water and then make offerings to God. These offerings were very significant as we consider what the Gospels tell us about Jesus: a basket of unleavened bread; drink and grain offerings; a lamb as a burnt offering; a ewe as a sin offering; a ram as a peace offering. And when we read the Gospels, although the order of events differs, we can see the same nazir requirements applying to Jesus.

Jesus began his ministry with his Baptism in water by John. Then he went off into the wilderness, not for the minimum 30 but for 40 days! And as Jesus developed in his ministry and understanding of God, his initial strict Pharisaic rules and regulations, along with his Nazarite background, eventually gave way to a new freedom and abundance of life based on Perfect, Sacrificial and Unconditional Love. Although the Gospels show that Jesus enjoyed a party and doubtless partook of wine, it was almost at the end of his life that he said that he would not drink wine again until he came into the Kingdom beyond death. As I think about that Last Supper with his friends, I wonder if he was he returning to the sense of security of his Nazarite roots before the inevitability of his arrest, trial and execution?

Let us also remember the parallels between the bread and wine, and Jesus. According to the Gospel accounts, Jesus took the wine during the Last Supper saying that in drinking it, his followers were remembering his blood that was to be shed. The Gospels also tell us that Jesus took the bread and broke it as a symbol of what was to happen to his body.

Thirty years after his execution, Jesus had developed in the minds and experiences of the Gospel writers who, by then, were interpreting him as the One who sacrificially offered himself as the Nazarite, and as the Lamb of God, the ewe of the sin offering, and the ram of the peace offering. This Jesus is the One who, according to our outdated creeds and doctrines, takes away the sins of the world. I am convinced that for Mark, Matthew and Luke, Jesus of Nazareth, so full of humanity, had become the 'nazir' – the consecrated one, set apart for God to use in a unique and special way; and when I take the bread and wine in Communion I remember Jesus as both the consecrated spiritual Nazarite and Jesus the geographic Nazarene who lived the fullness of humanity through which people experienced Divinity.

Luke 2: 1-38
The birth of Jesus

1 In those days Caesar Augustus issued a decree that a census should be taken of the entire Roman world. 2 (This was the first census that took place while Quirinius was governor of Syria.) 3 And everyone went to his own town to register. 4 So Joseph also went up from the town of Nazareth in Galilee to Judea, to Bethlehem the town of David, because he belonged to the house and line of David. 5 He went there to register with Mary, who was pledged to be married to him and was expecting a child. 6 While they were there, the time came for the baby to be born, 7 and she gave birth to her firstborn, a son. She wrapped him in cloths and placed him in a manger, because there was no room for them in the inn.

The Shepherds and the Angels

8 And there were shepherds living out in the fields nearby, keeping watch over their flocks at night. 9 An angel of the Lord appeared to them, and the glory of the Lord shone around them, and they were terrified. 10 But the angel said to them, "Do not be afraid. I bring you good news of great joy that will be for all the people. 11 Today in the town of David a Savior has been born to you; he is Christ the Lord. 12 This will be a sign to you: You will find a baby wrapped in cloths and lying in a manger."

13 Suddenly a great company of the heavenly host appeared with the angel, praising God and saying, 14 "Glory to God in the highest, and on earth peace to men on whom his favor rests." 15 When the angels had left them and gone into heaven, the shepherds said to one another, "Let's go to Bethlehem and see this thing that has happened, which the Lord has told us about."

16 So they hurried off and found Mary and Joseph, and the baby, who was lying in the manger. 17 When they had seen him, they spread the word concerning what had been told them about this child, 18 and all who heard it were amazed at what the shepherds said to them. 19 But Mary treasured up all these things and pondered them in her heart. 20 The shepherds returned, glorifying and praising God for all the things they had heard and seen, which were just as they had been told.

Jesus Presented in the Temple

21 On the eighth day, when it was time to circumcise him, he was named Jesus, the name the angel had given him before he had been conceived.

22 When the time of their purification according to the

Law of Moses had been completed, Joseph and Mary took him
to Jerusalem to present him to the Lord 23 [as it is written in
the Law of the Lord, "Every firstborn male is to be consecrated
to the Lord"], 24 and to offer a sacrifice in keeping with what
is said in the Law of the Lord: "a pair of doves or two young
pigeons."

25 Now there was a man in Jerusalem called Simeon, who
was righteous and devout. He was waiting for the consolation
of Israel, and the Holy Spirit was upon him. 26 It had been
revealed to him by the Holy Spirit that he would not die
before he had seen the Lord's Christ. 27 Moved by the Spirit,
he went into the temple courts. When the parents brought in
the child Jesus to do for him what the custom of the Law
required, 28 Simeon took him in his arms and praised God,
saying: 29 "Sovereign Lord, as you have promised, you now
dismiss your servant in peace. 30 For my eyes have seen your
salvation, 31 which you have prepared in the sight of all
people, 3 a light for revelation to the Gentiles and for glory to
your people Israel."

33 The child's father and mother marveled at what was said
about him. 34 Then Simeon blessed them and said to Mary, his
mother: "This child is destined to cause the falling and rising
of many in Israel, and to be a sign that will be spoken against,
35 so that the thoughts of many hearts will be revealed. And a
sword will pierce your own soul too." 36 There was also a
prophetess, Anna, the daughter of Phanuel, of the tribe of
Asher. She was very old; she had lived with her husband
seven years after her marriage, 37 and then was a widow until
she was eighty-four. She never left the temple but worshiped
night and day, fasting and praying. 38 Coming up to them at
that very moment, she gave thanks to God and spoke about
the child to all who were looking forward to the redemption
of Jerusalem.

Only two of our four Gospels, Matthew and Luke, have a genealogy for Jesus. In Matthew, the first of the two to be written, the genealogy is how Matthew opens his Gospel. Matthew has forty names but says that there were forty-two generations going back as far as Abraham; and an interesting thing, at least to me, is why Matthew's genealogy starts at chapter 1 v1, and yet Luke's genealogy does not start until ch 3. v 23?

Luke's genealogy has fifty-six names going back to Abraham, but then continues the list to twenty more names, going right back to Adam. Whether or not Luke used the name 'Adam' for a real person, as far as I am concerned, Adam is a metaphor for all humankind. Both genealogies cannot be right, but that is not the point because scholarship indicates that something else was at work in Luke's Gospel.

Following the scholarship of Goulder and Spong, it seems to me that in Luke's Gospel the genealogy is delayed so that it can coincide with the Sabbath teaching in the synagogue at the appropriate place in the Torah calendar of readings in Luke's synagogue. If you have followed this far, it will not surprise you that the end of the Torah reading that concluded the life of Jacob, is Genesis 46:8 – 27. It is here that you will find a four-generation genealogy of the descendants of Jacob and, if our contemporary Biblical scholarship is correct, it is this Sabbath reading that was shared by Luke with his version of the genealogy of Jesus!

Now, all of what I have said could be no more than circumstantial evidence. It could be a long list of nothing more than mere random coincidences. However, so many coincidences convince me that the Gospels were not written as literal history but as Midrash, mythology and fiction, based upon both the remembered events and sayings from the life of Jesus, and upon the Jewish approach in which contemporary parallels were made to the reading of the Torah and other stories in the synagogues.

If you choose to believe the Christmas stories as literal fact, then it is right for you to do so, and I bless you and encourage you in your understanding. However, there are other ways of understanding the Christmas stories, and to believe one or other way is not to make any of us more or any less a follower of Jesus. What we need to ask ourselves is this, "Beyond the stable; beyond the manger; beyond the miraculous conception; beyond the shepherds and the angels and the wise men; beyond all this, what is the central truth of the Christmas stories in Matthew and Luke?"

The central truth, no matter how we approach and interpret the Christmas stories is 'Immanuel - God with us.' The real challenge of the Christmas stories is not about how many of the events we can honestly say "I know that literally happened" – the real challenge of the Christmas Story is to look beyond the myths to the reality that the Perfect Love that is God is with us, and within us and about us; that the Perfect Love that is God comes to us every moment of every day, if only we have eyes to see, ears to hear and hearts open to serve. The Christmas stories are not for once a year, but Christmas is the reminder of the good news that the Perfect Love that is God is with us all the time, and will never leave us.

As I think about the story in Matthew's Gospel, there never was a guiding star, and if there was a comet, it came at least four years before the 'official' birth of Jesus. There never were three wise Gentile men, or Kings, who came to Jesus in the stable, and if there were such visitors, the only reason we say that there were three is that Matthew's version of the birth story records three gifts for the babe. There never were gifts of gold, frankincense or myrrh, but these were the creation of Matthew as he read the significance of these three gifts back into the event of the birth and life and death of Jesus 80 or 90 years after the birth event: gold for a king, frankincense for the Holy Son of God; and myrrh to embalm the crucified body of Jesus.

There never was a host of angels singing to the shepherds on the hillside. Shepherds never went to the stable, for if they did, and if there was this angelic choir, why didn't the innkeeper become aware of what was happening in the corner at that dirty, dark, smelly stable? And why didn't the whole of Bethlehem come alive to the news that the so-called King of Kings was born there in their midst? Or were their eyes blinded to the sight of angels and their ears deaf to the sounds of excited shepherds?

And there never was a Santa Claus. But of this I have no doubt, Jesus was born into a situation of deprivation, exploitation, oppression and poverty, as a subject of the Roman domination system. His later ministry was to challenge people to choose either the way of Caesar: the way of oppression and exploitation; or the way of Yahweh: the way of Perfect Love and sacrificial servant hood.

I have no doubt that when Matthew and Luke were writing their Gospels, probably 80 or 90 years after the birth of Jesus, they had an agenda for writing, and specific audiences to whom they were writing and who needed encouragement. They were not writing biography but they were writing a story of hope for those who felt hopeless.

They were not writing the real, actual historic truth of the birth event but they were writing to an oppressed people. They were writing to Jews who had been excluded from the synagogues and therefore from their entire Jewish historic religious culture because they dared to see Jesus as the fulfilment of the Jewish Testament; because they dared to see Jesus as the Messiah who would lead all people, both Jew and Gentile, to the worship of the Perfect Love that is God. They were writing to the Gentile Christians who were also now being persecuted by the Roman and the Jewish synagogue authorities; and it is not surprising to me to know that the interpretation of this Bethlehem story amongst the oppressed and the deprived and the poor of today's Third World countries is very different to our first world sanitized, tinsel covered, and gentle-Jesus-meek-and-mild interpretation of the birth of Jesus.

So what were the Gospel writers saying at the time of writing? The first thing was that God the Indwelling Spirit of Love will never abandon us, even in times of oppression, deprivation and poverty. The writers were giving them a renewal of hope because, in the story, the star led the wise men so that their hope of meeting the Messiah could be satisfied. It says to all people, and especially to the oppressed, the deprived and the poor, that there is good news; there is hope for now and for the future; that, one day, Mary's song will come true.

This is the song we call the Magnificat in which Mary says God will use his powerful arm to scatter those who are proud and will drag strong rulers from their thrones and put humble people in those places of power; that God will give the hungry good things to eat but will send the rich away with nothing. The story of the birth of Jesus is a story of immense hope for those who feel that life is hopeless.

Just as Archbishop Desmond Tutu has challenged in his question concerning which Bible is being read, when people say that Christianity and politics do not mix, I look at the Christmas stories and ask a similar question, "How can anyone look at the deep truth of the birth story of Jesus and say that Christianity and politics should not mix?"

Also, the star signified something of the awe-inspiring joy of people finding the Perfect Love that is God in their midst so that when the wise men in the story saw the star they celebrated with great joy. It is a joy that offers hope to the hopeless.

In the story it was a star that brought the people together. The wise men and the poor miserable shepherds from the hillside; the privileged and the underprivileged; the well informed and the uneducated; the cream of the crop and the lowest of the low: all were brought together around the babe Jesus. What a message of good news for an oppressed, deprived and poor people that in the Kingdom of God, brought to Christians by Jesus of Nazareth, there is no distinction based upon what or how much we know;

male or female; Jew or Gentile; black or white; or by any other words we choose to identify ourselves or to show to our status.

The truth of Christmas is that God the Indwelling Spirit of Unconditional, Sacrificial, Perfect and Compassionate Love accepts each one of us as we are so that we can live God's Kingdom in which there are no barriers; where all people are equal and receive their fair share of the riches of heaven and earth for us all. In the stories of the birth of Jesus written by Matthew and Luke, we see that some were prepared and willing to accept the babe who would become Jesus the Christ of the Church, and some were not ready; and the same situation applies to us today.

Although these events were not the historical reality of the birth of Jesus, it is in the explanatory fiction of the Bethlehem stories written by Matthew and Luke that we see that some missed the birth and, with it, the coming of this new manifestation of the Presence of God because they were not looking for it. On that night in Bethlehem it was 'business as usual' seeking a profi or enjoying the desires of life that they failed to find the God-Presence right there amongst them.

I am not saying that it is wrong to make money and to enjoy the pleasures of life; but the problem is how we do these things and what we do with them as a result. I wonder how much has really changed over these 2000 years since Matthew and Luke were saying to their readers, "Keep looking for Jesus, be ready for when he comes to you, search for him and you will find Him?" The message of Matthew and Luke was that God is on the side of all people, and can be found within all people, and comes to all people in others round about them, and we will only be aware of this if we are looking and we are serving. Matthew and Luke were saying to the oppressed, the deprived and the poor Followers of the Way of Jesus, "In spite of your present circumstances look beyond and see Jesus coming daily into your life and into your midst".

It is in following the values of the Kingdom, so fully demon-strated to us in Jesus, that this incomplete credit-crunched world will be helped to find its completion and its salvation from selfishness and greed. It is as I seek and serve Jesus the Christ Child who is born in all people that I find a renewed purpose that restores me as I seek and serve Jesus the Christ who comes to us day by day in the oppressed, in the deprived and in the poor.

I know that in saying some of these things I may have offended some people. That is not my intention. But to me, it doesn't matter that the birth story of Jesus may not be historically and factually true. The Eternal Truth of the birth stories of Jesus does not depend upon real wise men, real angels and real shepherds on the hillside.

But there are a number of fundamental contradictions when looking at the Matthew and Luke accounts of the birth of Jesus. It is obvious that they are not in agreement, and therefore they cannot both be historically reliable and correct. But then, neither was intended to be factually correct. The authors were trying to establish the line of Jesus the Jew as being central to the Jewish people. They were establishing the Jewish credentials of Jesus for both Jewish and Gentile Christians but they were not writing an historically accurate family tree.

Notice also that Luke has Mary and Joseph traveling from Nazareth in Galilee to go to Bethlehem in Judea for the so-called 'Roman census,' but Matthew's account looks as if the family is already living in Bethlehem. There is no Roman census in Matthew's Gospel, and, whereas Matthew has wise men following a wandering star, Luke has no record of these men or of their visit to King Herod. Matthew has Joseph taking flight with Mary and Jesus from the despotism of King Herod. The family goes as refugees into Egypt to protect the baby Jesus from the murderous actions of King Herod in which all the male babies are killed in an attempt to destroy the 'infant king'. But Luke has no verification of such an extraordinarily wicked story of the killing of the innocents and no record of Jesus spending his early years as a refugee in a foreign land.

There is further evidence that Matthew thought that the hometown of the 'Holy Family' was Bethlehem because he has the family returning from exile in Egypt intending to return to Judea, presumably to Bethlehem? However, being cautioned in a dream, they go instead to Nazareth in Galilee. This is all geographically confusing, and it doesn't end there!

There is still more to understanding the birth stories of Jesus! In Luke 2, Anna the old prophetess, saw the baby Jesus and announced to everyone that here was the one to set Jerusalem free. But what is really important about Anna is her own family lineage. She was the daughter of Phanuel from the tribe of Asher and the name Asher, in Hebrew, signifies "blessed and happy". But Phanuel is simply another way to spell 'Peniel' – the place where Jacob wrestled and met face to face with God! By adding, what to us may seem minor details, Luke is linking Jesus with aspects of the Hebrew Testament stories of Jacob. He is saying, "Jacob was one of our great leaders, one of our patriarchs – but Jesus is greater still".

The birth stories tell us more about the developing under-standings of Jesus and the thinking of the early Christian communities than they tell us biological and geographical facts concerning the birth of Jesus. The intention of Matthew the Jew was to make the links between Moses, the great Jewish leader, and Jesus. Remember that the infant Moses was also a refugee exiled in Egypt and was saved from the slaughter of the Jewish baby innocents at the hands of the Egyptian rulers and slave drivers. Is this just a coincidence of history or is this Jewish Midrash at work, taking the old and applying it to the new in Jesus, saying that no matter how great was Moses, Jesus was greater?

I am convinced that Matthew was not writing definitive history but was attempting to tell his readers that Jesus was the new Moses. And likewise, Luke was not writing definitive history but he was determined to make evident to his readers that God has a special concern for the stranger, the outsider, the social reject and the economic poor. Is it any wonder that Luke has the shepherds invited as God's first guests to visit the baby Jesus, long before the rich and famous were invited? Surely this is why Luke's Gospel is full of stories concerning the outsiders and social rejects, such as those with malevolent spirits; those in need of restoration to health from the sicknesses that damned them to live at a distance from the rest of their communities; drunkards, prostitutes, publicans, sinners and tax collectors; even the hated Samaritan foreigner condemned as being less than the equal of the Jew.

The Gospels of Matthew and Luke were written at a time when both Roman political persecution and Jewish synagogue authorities were rejecting and forcing Jewish and Gentile Followers of the Way of Jesus out of the synagogues and, in some cases, into fleeing as refugees. Both Matthew and Luke were writing, not for you or me, but for the disturbing times in which they and their followers lived.

I know that it has been argued that the Matthew and Luke accounts are not contradictory but that they are complementary, filling the gaps that the other author left out. But I think that the God of such gaps is another explanatory fiction of theologians and pulpit preachers who will not accept the fact that the Bible cannot be interpreted literally. No matter what we may think about the factual truth or otherwise of the stable, the angels, the shepherds and the wise men, the Christmas story is both a beautiful story and a Sacred story through which the Perfect Love that is God speaks to us. The Eternal Truth contained in the metaphors of those ancient stories is overwhelmingly real and speaks into the heart of life today for all who have ears to hear.

If we, as Followers of the Way of Jesus, live out the Truth of the birth stories recorded by Matthew and Luke then, perhaps, we should be pressuring the international community to do something more than it is doing now to bring the message that violence does not solve problems; that the way of the Perfect Love is the way of equality, justice and respect of difference; that the pain of forgiveness and the power of love can solve the causes and challenges presented by asylum seekers and refugees. The Eternal Truth of the birth stories of Jesus is that only the Unconditional, Sacrificial, Compassionate Love that is God can solve the continuing challenges of personal, national and international life today.

The birth stories of Jesus are about a young mother with a baby that could have been considered to be illegitimate, and said to have been born in the dirt and the grime and the foul smells of a cattle shed or horse stable, demonstrating the Indwelling Divine Presence having a deep compassion for the underprivileged, the demoralized, the oppressed and the destitute. The birth stories of Jesus are not excuses to eat, drink and be merry, but they are stories of blood, sweat and tears that challenge the Followers of the Way of Jesus to meet head-on all that turns the standards and ethics of this world the wrong way up.

I am not saying that the Followers of the Way of Jesus should be miserable. Far from it, because we are followers of the one who was uniquely fully human and through whom Divinity shone and still shines. But as I consider the birth stories of Jesus I have no need to believe in the un-biological or in the unbelievable to enable me to honor, to worship and to serve Perfect Love in this day and age.

In fact, to understand the Jesus birth stories as metaphor rather than as historic fact makes the message of Christmas far more meaningful to me than it ever did when I accepted the birth stories as factual Gospel Truth. To see the Truth of the birth stories of Jesus as metaphor rather than as biology or astronomy or geography is to set the Christmas story into the real world in which we live, a world of ecological pollution and global warming; of disease and hunger; of inequality and unfairness; a world of war and terrorism, most of which can be turned round for the better for all if there is the political will and the good actions of ordinary people to do something with and for the benefit of the poor, the oppressed and the exploited. Just as one example, to give fair shares to the poor will pull the carpet from out under the feet of terrorists and Jihadis. The message of the metaphor is to be lived out every day and it is to make an impact socially, psychologically, economically, politically, ecologically and theologically.

The birth stories of Jesus are the good news for us all that will transform the lives of individuals, communities, and of all God's people, no matter what color or sexual orientation they are, or where they live or by what creed they name their Gateway to the God encounter.

The birth stories of Jesus invite us to consider afresh our own need of a spiritual re-birth. It may surprise you that I use the language of the evangelical, but we all need that spiritual experience of being born again – not the once and for all, one-off experience that some Christians call 'conversion,' but we need the daily dying to self and to our selfish demands. Such a daily re-birth of putting others first, of loving unconditionally, will transform us little by little into the image, nature and character of God revealed to Christians in Jesus of Nazareth. This is the daily work of the Divine Indwelling Spirit.

But as we think of birth and re-birth, we can reflect upon the encounter of the adult Jesus with Nicodemus, a Pharisee and a member of the Sanhedrin. Nicodemus, steeped in Judaism, came to Jesus, the liberated Jew, who had discovered a new revelation of God that transcended the religion and its barriers. Nicodemus asked Jesus to help him understand what Jesus had discovered. The response of Jesus was that he needed to be born again. Quite rightly, Nicodemus responded with a perplexed, or was it a dismissive, "How can this be – I cannot go back into my mother's womb a second time?"

Traditional Christianity has presented this episode in terms of being born first time in the normal physical womb when the mother expels the babe into the freedom of the outside world, and the second birth being into the spiritual awareness of baptism or 'conversion' into Christianity. However, John Martin Sahajananda sheds new light on this conversation by inviting us to look beyond the physical re-birth and subsequently onto the traditional understanding of spiritual re-birth.

Sahajananda suggests that what Jesus discovered was that the Judaism in which he was birthed had, like all other religions, set up barriers as to who was in and who was out [i.e. Jew and Gentile]. Jesus of Nazareth had grown in his understanding of God so that he reached the point where Gentiles were no longer dogs and a Jewish man could talk openly to a Samaritan woman. Jesus had discovered that the One God of All was greater than the Jewish God and greater than all the gods of the Gentiles. Sahajananda suggests that Jesus was talking of Judaism being the womb of faith, when Nicodemus was still stuck on the physical aspect of returning to his mother's womb.

A whole new understanding of God opens up when the story of Jesus meeting with Nicodemus is put into the context of the second birth being the realization that it is necessary to be 'wombed' and born and nurtured within a religion and its associated culture; but then there is a further step in which we are to be 'birthed' out of that religion into what Ian Lawton calls 'Spiritual but not religious'. Sahajananda is rejecting the idea that this 'second birth' is about conversion from one religion to another. Instead, where Sahajananda is particularly helpful is in suggesting that this 'second birth' is out of all religious groupings into the glorious liberty of seeing that God is not on the side of one religion [usually the 'my' religion] and against the others. This second birth is the God-inspired realization that we all need the 'wombing' and nurturing within a religion, but then we need to go beyond the barriers created by the individual religions to the liberty of the Spirit that transcends all religions.

No longer will we have to serve religion but this second birth liberty makes religion serve us as we genuinely come to see that all people are united as sister and brother under the One God, and that we together have a responsibility to work together for the common good, peace, justice and equality, and for the future of Creation.

It remains important for Christians to be 'wombed' and nurtured, and celebrate the metaphorical birth stories of Jesus the Christ child. But we should also be experiencing the Truth of those birth stories in our own lives everyday, in all that we think and speak and do. The spiritual transformation that results from this experience is life in all its abundance, regardless of the circumstances that we have to face day by day; and that is something about which we can and should be joyful!

Yet we must not forget that the events surrounding the birth stories of Jesus are not unique to Jesus but happened before him and after him. For example, Brahmin scholars [equivalent to the wise men?] and a hermit seer, Asita, visited a special babe from the mountainside [equivalent to the shepherds on the hill side or to Simeon?] were present in the virgin [yes, virgin!] Birth stories of Gautama Buddha, somewhere between 563 and 483 B.C.E. Stars were understood as coded messages associated with greatness and often accompanied the birth of other great men, for example, Caesar Augustus six decades before the birth of Jesus.

I am certain that the birth of Jesus did not happen in the way described by Matthew and Luke but its truth is truly transformational and it really is the message that the world always needs to hear and to experience. And those who follow the Ways of Jesus are amongst the people who have the privilege and responsibility to be the Sacred metaphorical hands, the metaphorical ears and the metaphorical feet of God, not just for Christmas but for today and every day.

Chapter Two

Jesus' Ministry In Galilee

Luke 7:11-17
The widow of Nain

11 Soon afterward, Jesus went to a town called Nain, and his disciples and a large crowd went along with him. 12 As he approached the town gate, a dead person was being carried out—the only son of his mother, and she was a widow. And a large crowd from the town was with her. 13 When the Lord saw her, his heart went out to her and he said, "Don't cry." 14 Then he went up and touched the coffin, and those carrying it stood still. He said, "Young man, I say to you, get up!" 15 The dead man sat up and began to talk, and Jesus gave him back to his mother. 16 They were all filled with awe and praised God. "A great prophet has appeared among us," they said. "God has come to help his people." 17 This news about Jesus spread throughout Judea and the surrounding country.

Here we have the widow of Nain whose only son has died. Jesus met the funeral party weeping on its way to the burial. This would, in all probability, have been at dusk, the traditional time for Jewish burials. Perhaps not the whole city but certainly a very large number of local people had joined the procession in support of the widow who had no family left to care for her. With nothing left the future for this widow looked bleak. She would be condemned to being little more than an outcast, depending upon the generosity of others. This story occurs in no other Gospel, and therefore here we encounter again Luke's concern for the deprived and the outsider. Luke's Gospel records that

Jesus had compassion for the widow and raised her dead son to new life. And all the people were amazed and began to praise God for the miraculous and the mysterious event that has happened in their presence.

It is a wonderful story of compassion – but did it really happen? Is this part of the Christian mythology that built amongst the Followers of the Way of Jesus as they tried to describe the indescribable impact of Jesus upon them? And where have we heard this story before? Could this be another case of Midrash – taking stories from the Hebrew Scriptures and rewriting them and applying them to Jesus to demonstrate how wonderful and how important Jesus was amongst the greats of the Hebrew religion? So where is the story of the widow of Nain in the Hebrew Scriptures? It is in 1 Kings 17: 17 – 24.

17 Some time later the son of the woman who owned the house became ill. He grew worse and worse, and finally stopped breathing. 18 She said, to Elijah, "What do you have against me, man of God? Did you come to remind me of my sin and kill my son?" 19 "Give me your son," Elijah replied. He took him from her arms, carried him to the upper room where he was staying, and laid him on his bed. 20 Then he cried out to the LORD, "O LORD my God, have you brought tragedy also upon this widow I am staying with, by causing her son to die?" 21 Then he stretched himself out on the boy three times and cried to the LORD, "O LORD my God, let this boy's life return to him!" 22 The LORD heard Elijah's cry, and the boy's life returned to him, and he lived. 23 Elijah picked up the child and carried him down from the room into the house. He gave him to his mother and said, "Look, your son is alive!" 24 Then the woman said, to Elijah, "Now I know that you are a man of God and that the word of the LORD from your mouth is the truth."

The first Book of Kings was probably written just before the Babylonian exile, some 600 years before the life of Jesus. Both the first and second Books of Kings are histories – but often-mytho-logical histories. Luke is drawing the parallel between Elijah, that great Prophet of the Hebrew Scriptures, and Jesus, the latter-day Jewish prophet for all people. Luke is saying to the Jewish and Gentile Followers of the Way of Jesus, "Look how great Elijah was. Consider what wonderful things the Scriptures tell us Elijah did. But I tell you, no matter how great Elijah was, Jesus was greater still."

The young and only son of a widow dies, and Elijah takes the boy from the mother. The young and only son of a widow dies, and Jesus takes the boy from the mother. Elijah raises the dead son of a widow to new life. Jesus raises the dead son of a widow to new life. Elijah gives the boy back to his mother, alive. Jesus gives the boy back to his mother, alive. The widow, in response to the miracle says to Elijah, "Now I know that you are a man of God and that the word of the LORD from your mouth is the truth." The people, in response to the Jesus miracle say, "A prophet is here with us! God has come to his people."

To see this story of the raising to new life of the son of the widow of Nain as nothing more than myth and Midrash does not make the story a lie in the sense of truth and lies. According to John A.T. Robinson, one time Bishop of Woolwich, in his radical and wonderful book, *Honest to God*, written in 1963, "Myth has its perfectly legitimate and indeed profoundly important place. The myth is there to indicate the significance of the events, the divine depth of the history."

Myths contain insightful Truth, if only we have the eyes and ears ready to see and to hear the supreme reality implanted within the story. Marcus Borg has spoken of a Native North American storyteller who starts his tribal stories with: "I know that the story didn't happen quite like this, but I know that the story is profoundly true. "

Unless Christianity in this post-modern world moves beyond literalism and into exploring the Truth contained in the Midrash and in the myth, then Christianity will surely disappear from all but those who need the emotional crutch of a supernatural faith in which God is the Being who sits beyond the sky, intervening from time to time, blessing some and condemning others.

The raising of the son of the widow of Nain is a wonderful story that can bring new life to all, speaking as it does into the heart of life today – speaking of the Perfect Compassionate Love that is made known to us in Jesus of Nazareth, a Perfect Love that can support the widows and fatherless through the actions of ordinary people.

Luke 7: 38 – 50
Simon the Pharisee and the woman of ill-repute

38 And as she stood behind him at his feet weeping, she began to wet his feet with her tears. Then she wiped them with her hair, kissed them and poured perfume on them. 39 When the Pharisee who had invited him saw this, he said, to himself, "If this man were a prophet, he would know who is touching him and what kind of woman she is—that she is a sinner." 40 Jesus answered him, "Simon, I have something to tell you." "Tell me, teacher," he said. 41 "Two men owed money to a certain moneylender. One owed him five hundred denarii, and the other fifty. 42 Neither of them had the money to pay him back, so he cancelled the debts of both. Now which of them will love him more?" 43 Simon replied, "I suppose the one who had the bigger debt cancelled." "You have judged correctly," Jesus said. 44 Then he turned toward the woman and said to Simon, "Do you see this woman? I came into your house. You did not give me any water for my feet, but she wet my feet with her tears and wiped them with her hair. 45 You did not give me a kiss, but this woman, from the time I entered, has not stopped

kissing my feet. 46 You did not put oil on my head, but she has poured perfume on my feet. 47 Therefore, I tell you, her many sins have been forgiven—for she loved much. But he who has been forgiven little loves little." 48 Then Jesus said to her, "Your sins are forgiven." 49 The other guests began to say among themselves, "Who is this who even forgives sins?" 50 Jesus said to the woman, "Your faith has saved you; go in peace."

John Vincent, President of the British Methodist Conference in 1989, in his 1962 book, *Christ in a Nuclear Age*, wrote "... Christ is there. We can be with him or against him. We can look for him or be blind to him. The choice is ours."

Choices and discipleship can cost us dearly. For example, in the case of Oscar Romero, he made his choice to preach on behalf of the poor and he paid the supreme price. Here, in the Gospel story of Simon the Pharisee and an unnamed woman of ill-repute, possibly an adulteress, we have two people making choices. Simon does not welcome Jesus according to the custom of feet washing. Instead, the courtesies of the host are performed by this unnamed woman who has gatecrashed the party and is anointing Jesus with expensive perfume and washing his feet with her tears of remorse and drying his feet with her hair. Simon the Pharisee has invited Jesus to a meal but he has not acted as a host should have done. In ignoring the common courtesies of host towards a guest, Simon is treating Jesus with little respect. So I wonder why he has invited Jesus in the first place?

Perhaps I am reading too much into the text but I suggest that here is possible evidence that, in the early days of his ministry, Jesus himself may have been a Pharisee and a Rabbi. After all, he did keep himself apart from Gentiles and even called the Syro-Phoenician woman in Mark 7 and Matthew 15 'a dog' – a derogatory term of that time to describe Gentiles. But this incident may have been the turning point for Jesus in that he gradually saw that God's Love and Compassion was for all – not just for the Jews. Perhaps it was from this point that his ministry took a new direction of inclusiveness?

Perhaps Simon the Pharisee recognized Jesus as a fellow Pharisee but really wanted to know if Jesus was also a true prophet? After all, according to Luke's Gospel the news of what Jesus had been doing – speaking prophetically, healing the sick and raising the dead was spreading around the district. But Simon's seeking after the truth about Jesus is brought to a premature end when, in response to Jesus allowing the woman to come near him, Simon concludes, 'if this man really was a prophet he would know what kind of woman is touching him. He would know that she is a sinner.'

Simon the Pharisee was thinking like any right thinking Pharisee would have done. Pharisees kept themselves holy by separating themselves from all other Jews who did not maintain the strict Pharisaic way of living. In Simon's understanding, if Jesus had been a good Pharisee then he too would have rejected the woman and would not have allowed her to come anywhere near him. But in allowing this woman to do what she was doing proved, at least to Simon, that his guest was neither a good Pharisee nor a prophet of God. Simon the Pharisee was making his choice about Jesus, based upon an exclusivity of belief that imprisoned him within the traditions and teachings of his Pharisaic version of Judaism. These blinded Simon to the Truth standing in front of him that Jesus lived the inclusive and unconditional love that is God's Kingdom.

But in contrast, the woman of ill repute makes her choice to serve Jesus. Again I take poetic license, although John's Gospel account of this (or a similar incident) contradicts me! However, I like to think that this was the woman who was caught in the act of adultery and was facing stoning to death when Jesus arrived on the scene. The Pharisees and those men who felt threatened by a sinful woman, who was deemed to be the property of a father or husband, were going to execute her according to Mosaic Law. As Jesus stood between the woman and her accusers, notice that he did *not* say that the Law of stoning to death was wrong (a good Pharisaic Rabbi upholding the Law perhaps?) However, Jesus presented the would-be executioners with his reformation teaching that vengeance and so-called justice should give way to unconditional, compassionate love, forgiveness and acceptance. This is what has become for me the central message and teaching of Good Friday!

When thinking about this incident, why should a crowd of committed Pharisees listen to a homeless itinerant wisdom teacher coming to them from Nazareth from where nothing good is thought to come? Why didn't they stone Jesus as well as the woman as he stood between them and her? Unless, of course, Jesus already had considerable authority that overruled the other Pharisees, perhaps as a recognized Pharisaic Rabbi who had additional prophetic authority? Many who followed Jesus proclaimed that he spoke with authority, unlike the Pharisees and itinerant preachers of the time. And the response of Jesus to those who were about to stone this woman to death was, 'He who is without sin should cast the first stone.'

All that Simon sees is a sinful woman of low social standing. Simon cannot see that even the lowest of the low – those rejected as unclean and unworthy by the high-minded Pharisees who faithfully kept the Law of Moses – are acceptable to God just as they are. Jesus asks Simon to look beyond his prejudice to see in the woman a real Child of the Divine; and it is the woman's repentance and faith that saves her from her self and, hopefully, her way of life. Luke is pointing out that salvation does not come through simply keeping holy rules and regulations but it comes through remorse, compassion and love.

So what does this mean, for example, for Methodists and for the Methodist Church in Britain today? In 2007 it reviewed The

1993 Resolutions on Human Sexuality created at the 1993 Methodist Conference [see Appendix]. This remains an emotive subject but I firmly believe that the example of Jesus constantly asks us to look at the quality, commitment and depth of love, even if that is between two people of the same gender. We cannot ignore the Scriptures even though those who attack homosexuality as a heinous sin seem to lack the knowledge of just how insignificant the Scriptures make this as a subject for concern.

Jack Spong reminds us that being gay is not an illness to be cured, and that it is just the same as being born with red hair or blue eyes. It is a natural biological orientation. There are very few foundational texts for those who quote the Bible as stating clearly that homosexuality is wrong. Genesis 19 is often referenced in relation to Sodom and Gomorrah but a careful reading of the text will show that it is not homosexuality that is being condemned but gang rape.

1 The two angels arrived at Sodom in the evening, and Lot was sitting in the gateway of the city. When he saw them, he got up to meet them and bowed down with his face to the ground. 2 "My lords," he said, "please turn aside to your servant's house. You can wash your feet and spend the night and then go on your way early in the morning." "No," they answered, "we will spend the night in the square." 3 But he insisted so strongly that they did go with him and entered his house. He prepared a meal for them, baking bread without yeast, and they ate. 4 Before they had gone to bed, all the men from every part of the city of Sodom—both young and old—surrounded the house. 5 They called to Lot, "Where are the men who came to you tonight? Bring them out to us so that we can have sex with them." 6 Lot went outside to meet them and shut the door behind him 7 and said, "No, my friends. Don't do this wicked thing. 8 Look, I have two daughters who have never slept with a man. Let me bring them out to you, and you can

do what you like with them. But don't do anything to these men, for they have come under the protection of my roof."

As highlighted by Spong [in *Born of a Virgin*, p 8] what is worse, same sex relations, or Lot offering his two virgin daughters to be gang raped in place of the two angels sent to warn Lot to leave the city?

Then there is Leviticus 18:22: "It is disgusting for a man to have sex with another man". Taken out of its context that is a categorical statement, but we need to see it in the context of the rest of Leviticus chapter 18 where there are prohibitions against having sex with any close relatives; or against having sex with any of the wives of your father [note that polygamy was acceptable for a man, because women were a man's property just like sheep, goats and cattle, and the richer the man, the more wives he could have. But a woman had to maintain a monogamous relationship with one husband or else it was deemed to be adultery]. In the man's world of that time, life was designed to be extremely favorable to the men and less so to the women. There are fourteen other prohibitions against sexual relationships with relatives. These were common sense laws and prohibitions designed on health grounds to protect against the genetic disorders of sexual inbreeding.

The Book of Leviticus was probably written during the Babylonian Exile, and what was needed to ensure the Jewish people and the Jewish faith survived was procreational sex rather than recreational sex. Inevitably single sex relationships were condemned as they could not produce children. All of this is repeated again in Leviticus chapter 20 where the punishment for violation is stated as stoning to death. If today we were to keep to the Mosaic Hebrew laws of Leviticus chapters 18 and 20 we would run out of stones, and society would be decimated by the stoning to death of women, daughters, neighbors and friends! Indeed, the Christian Church would lose many a clergy member, including some of its Bishops and Cathedral Deans!

Those who attack homosexuality on the basis that it is an abomination to God 'because the Bible says so' must not ignore the fact that in the Hebrew Scriptures there are just three chapters that have anything to say about homosexuality. Likewise, in the Christian Scriptures, there are just three references: in Romans 1; 1 Cor. 6; 1 Timothy 1. So out of 1189 chapters in the 66 Books of the Bible, the Anglican Church is going to be split asunder on the basis of 'out of context' references in six chapters.

Now take the word 'justice' and you will find that appears in twenty-four chapters of the Bible. Or take the word 'love' and you will find that appears in some two hundred chapters of the Bible. So which is more important, justice and love, or the condemnation of homosexuality? It is so easy to cherry pick Bible verses to support our own understandings – and then to claim that we have the authority of the Bible to back us up!

Consider also Leviticus 11 where you find the Law of Moses in regard to which animals you may eat and touch, and those that have to be avoided. Have you ever eaten rabbit or pork? If so, you have broken the laws of God given to Moses and you are unclean and have to be purified. But when you look at the whole of Leviticus 11, much of it makes perfect sense on health grounds – 'don't allow dead animals to pollute your drinking water and don't eat of the meats that, in a hot climate, go bad in a short time.' The Mosaic laws are common sense health guidance – not legalistic laws to be cherry picked and applied to support our own prejudices against any particular individual or group of people.

Consider Leviticus 19 v 19: "Don't plant two kinds of seed in the same field or wear clothes made of different kinds of material". So, all gardeners who have broad beans growing alongside Brussels sprouts and carrots – let us get out the stones now! Or those who wear cotton and polyester blends – oh dear – get out the stones again!

Consider Leviticus 25 v 44: "If you want slaves, buy them from other nations or from the foreigners who live in your own country and make them your property". So, on the basis of Leviticus 25 v 44, William Wilberforce and the anti-slave traders were working contrary to the laws of the Hebrew God given to Moses. So was all that was celebrated in 2007 in the ending of the 19th century trans-Atlantic slave-trade, an abomination to God in the same way that homosexuality is, to some, an apparent abomination to God? If the Mosaic Law really is God's eternal and unchanging last word on such lifestyles then much of God's word has been disproved by science and genetics or compromised by the humble fridge freezer, and thus has become irrelevant, inhuman and unjust, and should be dumped on the scrapheap of history.

However, if we take the lead from Jesus, then the Mosaic Law has much to offer but it needs to be taken beyond the age and context in which it was written. It needs to be interpreted with the unconditional and compassionate love that is God, demonstrated so fully in Jesus of Nazareth, as he responded to the woman taken in adultery and to the woman who broke the jar of perfume over him and washed his feet with her tears of repentance and gratitude, and dried his feet with her hair. The depth of Perfect Love shown by Jesus does *not* just apply to some of our 'sins' – it applies to our 'sins'.

Luke 8: 26 – 39
The wild man of Gerasa

26 They sailed to the region of the Gerasenes, which is across the lake from Galilee. 27 When Jesus stepped ashore, he was met by a demon-possessed man from the town. For a long time this man had not worn clothes or lived in a house, but had lived in the tombs. 28 When he saw Jesus, he cried out and fell at his feet, shouting at the top of his voice, "What do

you want with me, Jesus, Son of the Most High God? I beg you, don't torture me!" 29 For Jesus had commanded the evil spirit to come out of the man. Many times it had seized him, and though he was chained hand and foot and kept under guard, he had broken his chains and had been driven by the demon into solitary places. 30 Jesus asked him, "What is your name?" "Legion," he replied, because many demons had gone into him. 31 And they begged him repeatedly not to order them to go into the Abyss. 32 A large herd of pigs was feeding there on the hillside. The demons begged Jesus to let them go into them, and he gave them permission. 33 When the demons came out of the man, they went into the pigs, and the herd rushed down the steep bank into the lake and was drowned. 34 When those tending the pigs saw what had happened, they ran off and reported this in the town and countryside, 35 and the people went out to see what had happened. When they came to Jesus, they found the man from whom the demons had gone out, sitting at Jesus' feet, dressed and in his right mind; and they were afraid. 36 Those who had seen it told the people how the demon-possessed man had been cured. 37 Then all the people of the region of the Gerasenes asked Jesus to leave them, because they were overcome with fear. So he got into the boat and left. 38 The man from whom the demons had gone out begged to go with him, but Jesus sent him away, saying, 39 "Return home and tell how much God has done for you." So the man went away and told all over town how much Jesus had done for him.

This is the story of the wild man, probably a Jew living in the Gentile Greek area of Decapolis on the eastern side of Lake Galilee, near to the town of Gerasa. To protect the community he was held in chains in the graveyard. The people, including Jesus, thought that he was possessed by demons. But just think about this story for a moment – is this another case of Luke writing mythology about Jesus?

If not, and if this event really did take place, then the story shows that Jesus was unfair, unjust and no more than an economic vandal. Jesus, according to the story, cast the demons out of the wild man and sent them to the pigs – unclean as far as Jews were concerned – and the pigs thundered off and leapt over a cliff taking the demons with them. Although the story shows that the Jewish wild man was cured, the actions of Jesus destroyed the livelihood of the pig owners and swine herders.This was sheer vandalism and an act of economic sabotage against people of a different religion and a different nationality. But this action is so totally out of character with the Jesus that I experience through the pages of the Christian Testament that I cannot believe that he was an economic vandal. Therefore, to me, this is another myth of Mark, Matthew and Luke; but the truth within the myth is sadly that we seem to never learn because this story is being repeated again today, for example, by the Israeli apartheid in the occupied lands of Palestine.

Luke 9: 1 – 6
Instructions for the apostles

[1]When Jesus had called the Twelve together, he gave them power and authority to drive out all demons and to cure diseases, [2]and he sent them out to preach the kingdom of God and to heal the sick. [3]He told them: "Take nothing for the journey—no staff, no bag, no bread, no money, no extra tunic. [4]Whatever house you enter, stay there until you leave that town. [5]If people do not welcome you, shake the dust off your feet when you leave their town, as a testimony against them." [6]So they set out and went from village to village, preaching the gospel and healing people everywhere.

The message from this story is clear. If we don't know where we are going; if we don't look and listen to the signs and the signals; if we don't heed the warnings and if we don't know how to get there, the impact can be disastrous, not just for us as individuals but also often for those round about us, and for those who depend upon us.

Can you imagine how the Apostles must have felt when Jesus made things far more difficult by saying:

... "And by the way, don't take anything for the journey..."
"What no food?"
"No, no food" replies Jesus.
"Not even a bag?"
"No, not even a bag," replies Jesus.
"And what about money?"
"No money either," says Jesus.
"Should we take an extra shirt in case we are gone a long time or in case it gets too cold?"
"No, you won't need an extra shirt," says Jesus, "All you need for the journey is a staff and a pair of sandals".

Let us put ourselves in the place of the disciples – honestly, would you or would I have said, "Fine, no problem... let's go for it: no food; no money to buy food; nowhere to sleep; no idea where we are going; no change of clothing; so we'll happily walk along the rocky roads - no problem; let's Nike it - let's just do it!"

Would you or would I just do it? But this was the way for missionaries at the time of Jesus. No mass media, only people with a message prepared to give up all material comforts for the sake of the message and for the sake of converting others to that message.

Up to now, the disciples have been onlookers and supporters but not totally committed to following the costly ways of Jesus. And in the same way, we are called today not to be content to be onlookers and mere supporters of Jesus, but we are called to be active as the hands and feet, as the voice of Jesus at this time and in this place, serving and loving others in the Name of Jesus. Such traveling missionaries then – and in some churches today – depend upon the hospitality of local people.

Jesus told the disciples to accept the first hospitality offered in a town and not to 'shop around' for the best quality hospitality to be offered to them. They were to be content with what they were offered and in return they were to share the love and message of Jesus. For most of us it is not the same today, and perhaps it shouldn't be, as we live in a different time and a different place. But the principle still applies – we are to be courteous and grateful, and live the life and love of Jesus towards all others here and now.

In verse 5 Jesus tells them that if any town refuses to offer hospitality and to accept them, they are to leave the town, making no fuss, not arguing or causing problems but symbolically wiping the dust from their feet. Jewish people like nothing better than a good argument. The Hebrew Testament is littered with stories of where Jews argued with God! And for missionaries refused hospitality, to simply walk away without argument, and merely wiping the dust from their feet as they left, would have given the people something to talk about and argue about for a while!

Though the disciples were conscious of great weakness, and it was made perfectly clear to them by Jesus that they were to expect no worldly comforts or advantages - in obedience to him, as Luke puts it in chapter 10:3, they went "as lambs to the slaughter". According to Luke, they told the people who would listen that they must repent of their wrong behavior and to turn to God. And the result? They did as Jesus had done before them - they preached and healed the sick. We may not be called to miraculously heal the sick or to cast out demons today, except by the power of healing love and compassion offered to one another, but we are called to live the life of Christ to love those who are unlovable, and to lead others by our example into a living awareness of the Indwelling Presence within all people.

My hope is that all Followers of the Way of Jesus will know where we are going and in whose presence we go, looking and listening to the signs and the signals of the age in which we live. My wish is that we will heed the warnings and commit ourselves to doing what we can to get the love of Jesus across to a deeply spiritual but non-religious world, one that increasingly rejects both the Church and its message of Jesus the Christ.

Luke 9: 28 – 36
The Transfiguration of Jesus

I do not expect people to need a lobotomy to attend worship. They should not leave their thinking abilities and their daily experiences outside the church door; and it is perfectly acceptable to come with their questions and their doubts as well as with those things of which they are certain. As people worship they should be invited to bring their understandings and questions of what kind of God, God is. The question attributed to Jesus, "who do you say that I am?..." is still a question that we all need to answer day-by-day; and a similar question should be asked concerning the Bible..."What do you say the Bible is for?"

28 About eight days after Jesus said this, he took Peter, John and James with him and went up onto a mountain to pray. 29 As he was praying, the appearance of his face changed, and his clothes became as bright as a flash of lightning. 30 Two men, Moses and Elijah, 31 appeared in glorious splendor, talking with Jesus. They spoke about his departure, which he was about to bring to fulfilment at Jerusalem. 32 Peter and his companions were very sleepy, but when they became fully awake, they saw his glory and the two men standing with

him. 33 As the men were leaving Jesus, Peter said to him, "Master, it is good for us to be here. Let us put up three shelters—one for you, one for Moses and one for Elijah." [He did not know what he was saying.] 34 While he was speaking, a cloud appeared and enveloped them, and they were afraid as they entered the cloud. 35 A voice came from the cloud, saying, "This is my Son, whom I have chosen; listen to him." 36 When the voice had spoken, they found that Jesus was alone. The disciples kept this to themselves, and told no one at that time what they had seen.

I am indebted to the Christian Science Monitor for this story, especially as it concerns my hometown of Poole in Dorset. On a warm day in August, 2005 Harvey Bennett dropped five light-weight plastic bottles into Long Island Sound, N.Y., watching as they drifted out of sight on the waves. Inside each, he'd placed a note asking the finders to let him know where they were at the time. Five months later, he received a letter from 'disgruntled of Bournemouth': "I recently found your bottle while taking a scenic walk on the beach by Poole Harbor. While you may consider this some profound experiment on the path and speed of oceanic currents, I have another name for it – litter! If you wish to foul your own nest, all well and good, but please refrain in future from fouling mine."

But the story doesn't end there. A few days later, *The Daily Telegraph* apologized for its countryman. Calling the finder "humorless" and "pompous," it wrote, "Mr. Bennett must be assured that not all Brits are like that. Most of us understand the distinction between litter and international communication."

We understand the distinction between litter and communication but what has that distinction to do with this reading in Luke 9, and what do you think is the truth of the story of the Transfiguration of Jesus?

Is the story of the Transfiguration 'litter' – in the sense of an untidy story that is past its sell-by date, written some 30 years or more after the event, but still annually celebrated by many churches as literal truth - an historically accurate record of what really happened to Jesus? Or is the story of the Transfiguration of Jesus a communication that contains Eternal Truth but was not written to convey factual or historical accuracy? To answer that we need to look deeper into this communication from the Gospel writers as another example of Midrash.

In the Hebrew and Christian Scriptures, mountains usually signified an important encounter with God - a place of supernatural revelation. Consider again the story of the Transfiguration of Jesus: Jesus took three of his followers with him as he climbed high into the mountain, probably Mount Tabor or Mount Hermon, and consider Exodus 24, written during the Babylonian Exile, where Moses took with him three followers high upon Mount Sinai. And what happened next in these parallel stories?

A cloud descended upon Jesus and his three followers as they stood high up on the mountainside, just as a cloud descended upon the mountain and enveloped Moses. Upon that mountain Jesus is completely changed, and the story says that the disciples witnessed that his clothes became much whiter, like a shining light, just as the followers of Moses looked up and are said to have witnessed God's glory covering the mountaintop like the light of a blazing fire.

In the story of the Transfiguration of Jesus, the disciples claim to have seen Moses and Elijah talking with Jesus. What happened to Elijah at the end of his life? In 2 Kings 2, probably written just before the Babylonian Exile and revised at the end of the Babylonian Exile, we read that Elijah was so close to God that God did not let Elijah die. Instead, it is said, that God sent a fiery chariot and swept Elijah away into heaven to live in God's presence forever.

In Deuteronomy 34, written during the Babylonian Exile,

Moses is said to have died and that his grave is unmarked, unknown and will never be found. A later Jewish tradition developed a Midrashic understanding that Moses was so great that God dealt with him just as God later dealt with Elijah. God did not let him die but instead took Moses to be with God without suffering death; hence, the grave of Moses will never be found because it does not exist!

Starting with Mark some 30 years after the death of Jesus, what were the Synoptic Gospel writers trying to communicate concerning the Transfiguration of Jesus? Both Mark the Jew, and Matthew, the most Jewish of all four Gospel writers, were steeped in Jewish religion and history and Midrashic tradition. Similarly there was Luke, the Gentile, with all the zeal of a convert who has found something so fresh and life-changing. What are these writers reading into the life of Jesus?

First, Moses and Elijah are enormous characters in the Jewish religion, history and tradition, but once again, these Gospel writers were saying that in Jesus they had found the One who is greater than both Moses and Elijah. Just as the fire and light of God's supernatural presence was shown to be with Moses and Elijah, so, in the Transfiguration of Jesus, there is the confirmation of greatness when the same fire and light of God's supernatural presence falls upon him.

Just as Moses and Elijah experienced something supernatural as they moved from life on earth into the eternal presence of God, so there was something supernatural in the death and spiritual resurrection of Jesus as he moved from life on earth into that same eternal presence of God.

Did Moses, Elijah and Jesus historically experience very similar things? In my opinion, the story of the Transfiguration of Jesus as told by Mark, Matthew and Luke is Midrash. It is not a literally true, historical event but nevertheless, there is immense spiritual truth in the stories of Moses, Elijah and Jesus.

When we study the Hebrew and Christian Scriptures, we

should set aside our western thought patterns that have, all too often, treated Scripture as literal and historic truth. It is this that causes the majority of people in Britain and Australasia, and increasingly in North America, to reject Bible stories as being unscientific and therefore untrue, and with it, the Christian God and the messages of the Christian Church are dismissed.

Biblical literalism is a travesty of what the Hebrew and Christian writers were doing. The Jewish hearers and readers would have had no confusion but to our western Gentile mindset, too many Christians for far too long have taken the Gospel writers at face value, as giving us literal truth and historical accuracy. By interpreting the Scriptures in that way, we have misunderstood and misrepresented the Jesus of history. We have corrupted the very heart of the Hebrew and Christian Testaments.

Why is all this important to us in these post-modern days in which we live? Why shouldn't we just accept the Gospel stories at face value as they are written? Why complicate faith with Biblical scholarship? Why shouldn't we just simply close down our minds and believe the unbelievable and the unscientific?

We cannot go on like this, because literal interpretation of the Scriptures: Creation in 6 days; Adam and Eve and a snake and a tree; dry bones coming alive again; living in the belly of a large fish for three days; a lion's den and a fiery furnace; a wandering star - it is the literal interpretation of what is metaphor and Midrash that is killing the Church in our times and chasing away people who are seeking the spiritual but who cannot believe the unbelievable and the unscientific as seemingly presented by the Christian Church. Faith has nothing to do with believing the unbelievable, and the sooner we study the Scriptures with our Enlightened post-modern understandings, contemporary Biblical scholarship and the Jewish Midrashic style of the writers of those Scriptures, then the sooner we will rediscover the authentic message of Jesus and of the early writers and followers of the

Way of Jesus. In approaching the Bible in this way it offers a revitalized message for today's skeptical, rejecting and dismissive generation.

As I study the Hebrew and Christian Scriptures in the Jewish Midrashic style rather than through the eyes and experiences of Gentile literalists, I am discovering many new and exciting things about the Bible, the Sacred and my faith as a Follower of the Way of Jesus.

There is a similar Eternal Truth in 2nd Isaiah chapter 43, written immediately after the end of the Babylonian exile. This contains a reading in which the Lord is said to have spoken, 'Forget what happened long ago. Do not think about the past. I am creating something new. There it is! Do you see it? I have put roads in the desert, streams in thirsty lands.'

This is both metaphor and a Midrashic truth. God was not really out there in the desert with his tractors and giant earth-movers, cutting new roads across the wilderness, any more than God was creating new streams in the desert places so that thirsty people could drink. But here was 2nd Isaiah looking back into the stories and traditions of the Jewish people, including those of the slavery in Egypt and of the 40 years wandering aimlessly around the desert under the leadership of Moses. 2nd Isaiah was looking back at the recent experiences of Exile in Babylon; and into this new situation, as the people are released from Babylon and allowed to return home, 2nd Isaiah is saying "forget the past, you can do nothing about it – instead, look forward, for God is doing something new…"

2nd Isaiah was preaching hope to a worried people who were setting out on their journey 'home', not knowing what desolation would meet them back in Jerusalem, or what another 40 years of aimless wandering could do to them. 2nd Isaiah was saying "there is a new way across the desert wilderness experiences – a way that will give direction for those prepared to step out and take chances, and this new way will take us by streams of water so that the thirsty can drink until our thirst is quenched." Some would have been reluctant to leave Babylon – the devil of captivity you know being better than the devil you do not know waiting for them in Jerusalem.

In a similar way, the Church and Christians need to move on from the past and let go of the killing literalism of the Gentiles. In my opinion, we need to look to the radical and progressive message that has been with us for at least two centuries, but particularly since 'The Honest to God' controversy of 40 years ago. This is the message that will give a new direction to people who remain in the Church, along with their doubts and uncertainties. It is also a message that may speak afresh to those who have abandoned the Church because they can no longer believe the unbelievable and the unscientific, and to those outside of the churches who are seeking a real spirituality without organized institutional religion. The message of 2nd Isaiah is to forget the past and look forward with a new understanding of God the Divine Presence within us all – no longer seeing God as the Old Man above the sky or as the Master Chess Player arbitrarily handing out blessings and curses.

Is the message of our faith in Jesus one of litter that makes sense to fewer and fewer people, or is it a genuine communication that begins to make sense to us and to others? Are we people who despair as we look upon the Christian Church, seemingly disappearing from post-modern Europe and increasingly challenged in North America, and can only ask 'What is happening?'

Or are we amongst those who deny the slow death of the Christian Church in our day by simply hanging on – interpreting the Scriptures and the life of Jesus as we have always done through our killing literalism?

Or are we amongst those who will help to make things happen by rediscovering the real Jesus through metaphor and Midrash, so that we have a new and vibrant understanding of Jesus, leading to a genuinely fresh expression of faith and of Jesus that we can share with all?

Asking honest questions of our faith is not wrong, and reading Scripture with the creativity of metaphor and Midrash will be our keys to future church growth and Kingdom building. In God's name, we need something new and fresh and vibrant to communicate to the world around us.

Luke 9: 49 – 50
For or against Jesus

⁴⁹"Master," said John, "we saw a man driving out demons in your name and we tried to stop him, because he is not one of us." ⁵⁰"Do not stop him," Jesus said, "for whoever is not against you is for you."

Several Bible stories directly contradict themselves when written by different people at different times. For example, in 1st Isaiah 2 and Micah 4, both written in the 8th century before Jesus, when the people were free of captivity and slavery, these prophets wrote, 'You shall beat your swords into ploughshares.' And yet, in the 5th century before Jesus, and just after the release from Babylonian captivity, when the world of the Jews was again very threatening - Joel wrote, 'You shall beat your ploughshares into swords.'

Was there really a complete reversal in God's thinking across a span of 300 years? If God is understood as the all-powerful above the skies then, on this evidence, God is fickle and ever-changing and therefore cannot be trusted as the literalists and fundamentalists proclaim. Or something else was at work in the contexts of the writers and the writings of the Scriptures. Once again, that something else, as far as I understand it, was that the writers were writing of their experiences of their struggle with God the Indwelling Spirit working in and through the events of their lives to make their writings sacred for them. It was not God somewhere out there taking the hands and minds of the writers and dictating some unchanging and unchangeable word for all time.

Another example is found in Luke 9:49 and 50 where we have Luke's version that was originally from the pen of Mark [9:38-40]: Jesus says, 'Anyone who isn't against us is for us.' Think about it carefully. Surely, this undermines all the arguments of Christian literalists and fundamentalists who make God's unconditional love conditional upon believing a set of creeds and doctrines? Such literalism and fundamentalism are outrageous because they exclude people by saying who is in and who is out of God's Kingdom. No religious group – be it Christian, Muslim, Jew, Hindu, Sikh or whatever – no group can claim to have the only and the whole truth and nothing but the truth, and that those who disagree are wrong and condemned to eternal damnation and oblivion. To claim exclusive rights over the understanding and interpretation of God is arrogance beyond belief.

Think again about Luke's saying attributed to Jesus, 'Anyone who is not against us is for us.' To Luke the outsider, this would have meant Jew, Gentile and Greek, and perhaps even leading members of the Roman Empire? 'Anyone' – and doesn't that mean 'every one' - who is not actively against us is for us! And if that same statement holds true today, then think carefully about what it means. If a Jew, Muslim, Sikh, Hindu or whatever is not against us as Christians – if any who respect our faith because we also respect their faith and are prepared to work together with us in living and building God's Kingdom, then they are not against us – they are people with whom we have much in common and we should willingly share the task of living God's Kingdom.

But think again about those Christians who reject a progressive understanding of God as not being the all-powerful interventionist 'out there', maybe such Christians have less in common with us than some other religious people, no matter what name they give to their Gateway to God? But I still need to treat all people, even those literalists and fundamentalists who reject me and my theology, with respect even though respect may not be reciprocated.

Consider again the context of the times in which the Gospels were written. The Gospel of Mark was probably written in Rome in the mid-7th decade to early 8th decade C.E. Mark is usually thought to have been Peter's interpreter in Rome, and as a result of the executions of Peter and Paul, he wrote down all that he could remember Peter telling about the life and ministry of Jesus. This is most important background information, because Mark's Gospel was written in the midst of turmoil and persecution, and subsequently became a primary source for both Matthew's and then Luke's Gospels, both of which were also written in times of turmoil and persecution arising from military occupation and expulsion from the synagogues.

History tells us, probably erroneously, that in 64 C.E. Emperor Nero supposedly fiddled while Rome burned. And whom did Nero blame and subsequently persecute? The Jews in Rome, whom he thought were threatening to rebel just as the Jews were threatening to do in Palestine. As Mark was the earliest Christian Testament account written, I think that his version is the closest to those statements that Jesus might have made.

History also suggests that many of the Followers of the Way of Jesus at that time were Jews and were still worshipping in the synagogues. So Jewish Followers of the Way of Jesus were counted as Jews and therefore open to Nero's persecution in which death was not by crucifixion but by being burned as human torches. According to the tradition and mythology, Nero, the musician and actor, thought that this aptly reflected the crime of setting fire to Rome. History also tells us that the Palestinian Jewish rebellion against Roman occupation commenced in 67 C.E., resulting in a crushing defeat and the destruction of the

Jerusalem Temple in 70 C.E. It is in this similar context of persecution that the author of Mark was writing and two to three decades later both Matthew and Luke were writing. It is a context of looking over one's shoulder to see who was coming. Yet the advice given in Mark 9 v 40 and Luke 9 v 50 was, 'Anyone who isn't against us is for us. It is a statement of trust within a threatening and hostile world. It is a message for us today in a world that is violent, and where so often the news is dominated by acts or terrorism or students gunned down by fellow students across the campuses of the United States and Europe.

But let us also consider the Gospel attributed to Matthew, probably written between 80 and 90 CE in Caesarea Maritima. Matthew's context was also the aftermath of Roman defeat and ongoing persecution from fellow Jews in which those who did not follow Jesus, as they tried to hold onto the purity of their exclusive and ancient religion, were expelling the Jewish and Gentile Followers of the Way of Jesus from their synagogues.

This purity could not be allowed to weaken or change Judaism owing to the teaching of Jesus, or by the life-style of his Jewish and Gentile Followers whose sense of community and of turning the other cheek was perceived to be a threat to orthodoxy and to the future of Judaism. Even though the Gospels of Matthew and Luke were written in the context of persecution Matthew chapter 12 v 30 has Jesus saying the exact opposite of Luke 9:49 and 50, 'If you are not on my side you are against me.' Is this really the statement of an unchangeable God or is it simply that the context of the writing has changed and here is Matthew trying to protect his followers from the harmful impact of persecution and exclusion?

And could it be that Matthew's community was losing sight of the inclusive barrier-breaking message of Jesus? It is possible that Matthew's community was undermining the earlier radicalism of the followers of Jesus? For here Matthew seems to be using the same argument that the leaders of the synagogue were using to expel the Followers of the Way of Jesus. But this time God is claimed to be on the side of the Followers of Jesus and against those Jews who Matthew, more than any other Gospel writer, condemns as responsible for the death of Jesus. It is Matthew alone who has the story of the Jews before Pilate screaming for the death of Jesus. And when Pilate says 'I find no fault in Him,' Matthew has the Jews shouting 'We and our own families will take the blame for his death.' It is Matthew who most enthusiastically encourages the Followers of the Way of Jesus by saying that the religious institutional Jews had forfeited their own birthright as the Chosen Children of God because they had rejected Jesus and accepted his blood on their heads in perpetuity.

For Matthew and his followers those who were Christians had become the new Chosen People of God and the New Jerusalem. It is this Matthew passage above any other passage of the Christian Testament that has resulted in the most appalling Gentile persecution of Jews down the millennia with the greatest outrage of all being the Nazi Holocaust. It seems to me that Matthew more than the writers of the other Synoptic Gospels [Mark and Luke] wanted to get closer to the Romans perhaps to reduce the level of persecution against the Christians, proclaiming, "we are not Jews – we are Christians!"

But Matthew and Luke later also wanted to distance their communities from the religious institutional Jews. Consider the story of Jesus on Calvary's Cross – who is it who is screaming abuse at Jesus? Fellow religious institutional Jews! But who recognizes Jesus as God's Son? It is a Roman centurion! All three synoptic Gospels have this story, but Matthew goes a stage further towards Rome and against the religious institutional Jews. Matthew even has Pilate's wife warning Pilate not to harm Jesus 'the righteous one.' As I study the Scriptures, either Jesus is very fickle and changes his mind from one extreme to the other, or there is a contradiction here in these 'poles apart' statements about who is for and who is against us. This is not a Jesus problem, but the result of the Gospel writers having different agendas and different constituencies to whom they were writing.

Turning to the Gospel of Luke: tradition says that there were two great Jewish leaders of the Followers of the Way of Jesus in Antioch – Peter evangelized there and Paul taught about Jesus in the synagogue. This is where Paul first identified a distinct group of Followers of the Way of Jesus who were worshipping within the synagogue. In recognition of this group, Paul coined the term 'Christian.'

It is thought by many Bible scholars that Luke had been an early companion of Paul. Even into the 9th decade, when Luke was writing his two-part account of Jesus and the life of his early Church community, Antioch probably remained a place of welcome for Luke. But Luke's Antioch was still under Roman occupation and the Followers of the Way of Jesus had been expelled from the synagogues, so it could not have been entirely comfortable for Luke or for his community.

And what about the Gospel attributed to John? This Gospel was probably written around 100 C.E. in Ephesus, by which time the Followers of the Way of Jesus in Ephesus had been expelled from the synagogues. So how does John's Gospel interpret and present Mark's 'anyone who is not against us is for us'? It doesn't! The writer of John's Gospel completely ignores this saying. So my conclusion is that the writer of John's Gospel either chose to ignore the other three Gospels or had no access to them and therefore knew nothing of the saying.

What does the Gospel of Thomas have to say? Thomas never made the top four Gospels when 300 years later Athanasius decided which letters and Gospels should be in the Christian Testament and which should be excluded. Scholars are divided, but on the evidence I think that the Gospel of Thomas was probably written before Paul's letters and before the other four Gospels in our Christian Testament. It may even have been a source for Mark's Gospel but that is a debate for another occasion.

Thomas has the sayings immediately before and after Mark and Luke's 'Anyone who is not against us is for us' and 'Anyone who is not for us is against us' in Matthew, but Thomas completely ignores anything like these sayings. So Thomas, probably written closer to the time when Jesus may or may not have said any of these words, has no record of these sayings at all. So, did Jesus ever say anything remotely like the Mark or Luke statements or even something remotely like the Matthew corruption of the Mark and Luke? And if he did, which is right, Mark and Luke or Matthew?

All I can do is look at these contradictions and inconsistencies and the likely evidence of history and conclude that the nature of the Divine that I understand and experience in Jesus is more likely revealed in Mark's version and repeated by Luke, rather than in Matthew's. This has implications for the way in which we treat and work with all people who are prepared to work with us. It has a major impact upon how we perceive the extremist Muslims associated with Al Qaeda terrorism throughout the world and the extremist Muslims in places such as Pakistan, Afghanistan and Iraq, and in the National Health Service in Britain in June 2007 when Muslim doctors carried out an act of terrorism at Glasgow Airport.

Although one day leaders of nations will have to talk with Al Qaeda, at present we cannot work with them or accept that what they do is in the name of the One God of All people. But especially within the context of the violent and hate-filled world in which we live, the Mark and Luke saying should impact positively upon our attitude towards the vast majority of peaceful Muslims who, in the West, are as affronted and appalled as we are by the violence and destruction inflicted in the Name of Allah and of the Prophet Mohammed [peace be upon him] here and elsewhere.

Chapter Three

Jesus Goes From Galilee To Jerusalem

Luke 9: 51-62
The Samaritans reject Jesus

51 As the time approached for him to be taken up to heaven, Jesus resolutely set out for Jerusalem. 52 And he sent messengers on ahead, who went into a Samaritan village to get things ready for him; 53 but the people there did not welcome him, because he was heading for Jerusalem. 54 When the disciples James and John saw this, they asked, "Lord, do you want us to call fire down from heaven to destroy them?" 55 But Jesus turned and rebuked them, 56 and they went to another village. 57 As they were walking along the road, a man said, to him, "I will follow you wherever you go." 58 Jesus replied, "Foxes have holes and birds of the air have nests, but the Son of Man has no place to lay his head." 59 He said, to another man, "Follow me." But the man replied, "Lord, first let me go and bury my father." 60 Jesus said, to him, "Let the dead bury their own dead, but you go and proclaim the kingdom of God." 61 Still another said, "I will follow you, Lord; but first let me go back and say good-by to my family." 62 Jesus replied, "No one who puts his hand to the plough and looks back is fit for service in the kingdom of God."

Here we have the Samaritan rejection of the disciples and of the message of Jesus. As always it is essential that we understand the context and background to the writing of the text. As we do so it may become a little clearer as to why the Middle East continues to be a cauldron of violence and political insecurity. It is bedeviled by long memories and histories written and interpreted by the many different factions. One of the major problems for inter-religious or inter-ethnic wars across the world and across all times is that we cannot change history – we can only interpret it. Often such interpretation prolongs rather than solves the problem.

As I approach this story of the Good Samaritan there are two basic questions for me: The first, 'Even at the time of Jesus, why did the Jews and the Samaritans hate each other so much?' And the second, 'How far back does the hatred go?'

Although the 600 - 700 Samaritans who are alive today reject most of the Hebrew Scriptures, they still share with Jews the Torah, the Law of Moses contained in the Pentateuch, in Genesis, Exodus, Leviticus, Numbers and Deuteronomy. But the historical hatred can be traced back 2000 years before Jesus, back to Abraham.

In Genesis 12:6 and 7 we read of Shechem, the first place that Abraham, Sarah and Lot stopped when they entered the foreign land of Canaan. It was there that Yahweh God is said to have reconfirmed the Covenant made with Abraham at Harran concerning Jewish possession and ownership of Canaan, taken by force. And it will be no surprise that modern day Israel is part of what was Canaan.

Shechem became the first Israelite capital city and much later the main city linking Galilee in the north with Jerusalem in the south. At the time of Jesus, and even to this day, the Samaritans claim that the original Temple for Yahweh God was on Mt Gerizim Bethel and not on Mt Ebal. [And as an aside, the existence of a temple on Mt Gerizim was confirmed by the independent historical writer Josephus, in his *Antiquities of the Jews* written in 93 and 94 CE. Josephus stated that the later built Jerusalem Temple was similar to the Temple that was built on Mt Gerizim].

Be that as it may, after the Israelites had conquered and ethnically cleansed Canaan, Joshua brought the tribes back to Shechem to renew their commitment to Yahweh God. But from those days, and even at the time of Jesus, the Samaritans were claiming that the earlier religious leaders had misled the Jews and taken them away from the assigned Holy Path for Yahweh's Chosen People. The Samaritans accused Elijah of acting against the will of God by relocating the Holy Place from Mt Gerizim to Shilo. That was a direct attack upon one of the most important prophets of Judaism.

The action of Elijah and the reaction of the Samaritans was enough to engender hatred between both communities – but there was more. King Solomon, the son of the murderer King David and the adulteress Bathsheba, was born in Jerusalem about 1000 years before Jesus. Solomon became king of all Israel, including Samaria in 970 BCE. He reigned for 42 years and although Solomon had inherited a thriving nation from his father, Solomon's policies of disproportionate taxes and treating labor as almost slavery, incensed his people. Solomon also took many foreign wives and towards the end of his life he began to vacillate as a follower of Yahweh God. When Solomon died the ten Northern Kingdoms rebelled against Rehoboam his son and made Jeroboam their king.

The rebellion brought about the Southern Kingdom called Judah, but later renamed as Judea, with its capital Jerusalem; and just to complicate it, there was the Northern Kingdom named Israel, with its capital a fortified hill top city of Samaria! Later still, by the time of Jesus, this Northern Kingdom had been renamed 'Galilee.'

But, not surprisingly, the Jewish interpretation of the Samaritan history is very different. It is claimed that the Samaritans are not related to the Jews at all but that they were foreigners resettled by the Assyrians into Shechem, who then took to themselves aspects and understandings of the Jewish

Torah.

However, in the face of these conflicting interpretations of history, there is scientific evidence to verify the Samaritan claim that they are descended from Jacob, just as the Jews are descended from Jacob. In 2004, a group of scholars led by Peidong Shen, a specialist in genome research, studied the DNA of 640 Samaritans still living in the Palestinian West Bank. What they discovered was that the surviving Samaritan males have Y-chromosomes that closely match the Y-chromosomes of Jewish males. It is beyond my understanding but Shen and the other scholars concluded that the DNA evidence linked the surviving Samaritans directly to the Jewish priests who were not taken into Assyrian captivity 700 years before Jesus. Shen also states that the DNA shows that these descendants married Assyrian women, reflecting the Assyrian policy to wipe out the cultures of conquered nations by assimilating them through marriage. This ancient story, further complicated by the rivalry between Arab and Jew, continues to be played out today in the violence of the Palestinian West Bank where Shechem is now known as Nablus, a town that often features in the tragic news of Israel/Palestine.

In Luke 9: 51-62 we find Jesus setting his face to go to Jerusalem. The journey would take him through Samaria probably on the Shechem/Nablus road. And like the Jews, the Samaritans were looking for the Messiah, and perhaps they were beginning to see Jesus in that context, as one of them coming from Galilee, the old Northern Kingdom? After all, the news of Jesus and of what he was doing was not a million miles away. Samaria was only 25 miles to the south of Nazareth, and 20 miles from Nain where, according to Luke, Jesus had recently raised the dead son to life. Such news, if it were true, would travel fast even in those days!

Now the news was that Jesus was on his way to Samaria. He had even sent an advance party of disciples before him! If Jesus were to be their Chosen One then he would be putting the

Samaritans back where they believed they rightfully belonged, replacing the Jews as the heirs of Yahweh's Kingdom promises. But as soon as they realized that Jesus was going to pass them by on his way to Jerusalem, they turned against his followers, against his message and against him.

Remember that Luke was not writing history but a story based upon oral and written accounts of the life of Jesus. The order in which Luke selected his stories of Jesus is important. In Luke's order of things this is not the first time that Jesus had been rejected. In Luke 4 his hometown people in Nazareth rejected Jesus. He had just read the Isaiah Scripture 'the Spirit of the Lord in upon me' and the people wanted to kill him.

Then in Luke 6 Jesus declared the Blessings and Troubles for those who follow his way. This is immediately followed by Jesus clearly stating that we are to love our enemies, and that included Jesus loving the people of Nazareth who wanted him dead. Luke 6 continues with Jesus warning his followers not to judge others and then, in Luke 7 Jesus is rejected by Simon the Pharisee. All of this is Luke's literary device leading to Luke 9 and the rejection by the Samaritans. And yet, in Luke 10, Jesus is telling the story of the Good Samaritan, holding up the actions of this hated foreigner as praiseworthy, and criticizing the Jewish religious hierarchy for its attitudes towards one of its own people left as dead in the gutter.

So one of the messages for me is that I should not judge from a position of prejudice or to seek revenge. I am called to bless instead, even when I am rejected for upholding progressive theology. Luke hammers this message home. He writes that when the disciples were rejected by the Samaritans they wanted to call down the same heavenly fire that Elijah is said to have called upon in 2 Kings 1 to destroy the military officer and 50 men sent to take him to Ahaziah, King of Israel. It was the same heavenly fire that Elijah called upon again to destroy another military officer and 50 more men. And the place where this Elijah incident happened? Would it be a surprise if I said that it was again in Samaria? More Midrash perhaps?

From personal experience, Luke the outsider knew that there was a cost to following the Ways of Jesus. He summed up this cost in those three little episodes in Luke 9:57-62:

> 57 As they were walking along the road, a man said, to him, "I will follow you wherever you go." 58 Jesus replied, "Foxes have holes and birds of the air have nests, but the Son of Man has no place to lay his head." 59 He said, to another man, "Follow me." But the man replied, "Lord, first let me go and bury my father." 60 Jesus said, to him, "Let the dead bury their own dead, but you go and proclaim the kingdom of God." 61 Still another said, "I will follow you, Lord; but first let me go back and say good-by to my family." 62 Jesus replied, "No one who puts his hand to the plough and looks back is fit for service in the kingdom of God."

I am of the opinion that even though the Samaritans rejected Jesus, he continued his vision of transforming religious Judaism, and by living his developing message of reconciliation, he persevered in his politico-religious attempt to bring together again the two kingdoms of the descendants of Jacob. So beyond the stories of Samaritan rejection and the cost of following Jesus, the Eternal Truth of reconciliation shines through again and again.

To live by the demands of God's Kingdom will cost me. Discipleship is not going a happy-clappy, easy ride through life. The Way of Perfect Love is the way of justice and peace. It is not the way of vengeance, even when others reject me or try to harm me. It applies also to the few who are perceived to be our enemies in the aftermath of America's 9/11 and the subsequent bombings in London, Madrid, Bali and elsewhere. It is the Eternal Truth that I am to live forgiveness, unconditional love and reconciliation towards all people and in all circumstances, and especially towards those in minority communities. Such Truth should determine how I live in my home and family, in my church and local community.

It should underpin the policies of any Government of any country. It is the Eternal Truth that dialogue and moderation are those primary tools of Kingdom living that can transform the politics and economic well-being of all in Iraq, Israel/Palestine, Afghanistan, Kenya, Zimbabwe. And as much as I disagreed with Tony Blair, especially over involvement in Iraq, I hope that he is as successful in the Middle East as he was in Northern Ireland in bringing peace, justice and prosperity for all in Israel/ Palestine and beyond. However, in Northern Ireland Blair was dealing with 400 years of interpreted and re-written history but in the Middle East he is dealing with 4000 years of interpreted memories and stories.

What a different world this would be if we all lived according to these Truths as demonstrated to us by Jesus of Nazareth! What a different world we would be living in if all people could put their hands to the plough to create the future, without looking back at their interpretations of history. In Luke 9:62 we are reminded that it is in living and working not in the past but in the present and in looking to the future, that the Kingdom of God is served. It is another of those Gospel imperatives.

Luke 10: 25 – 37
The Parable of the Good Samaritan

25 On one occasion an expert in the law stood up to test Jesus. "Teacher," he asked, "what must I do to inherit eternal life?"

26"What is written in the Law?" he replied. "How do you read it?"

27 He answered: "Love the Lord your God with all your heart and with all your soul and with all your strength and

with all your mind;" and, "Love your neighbor as yourself."

28 "You have answered correctly," Jesus replied. "Do this and you will live."

29 But he wanted to justify himself, so he asked Jesus, "And who is my neighbor?"

30 In reply Jesus said, "A man was going down from Jerusalem to Jericho, when he fell into the hands of robbers. They stripped him of his clothes, beat him and went away, leaving him half dead. 31 A priest happened to be going down the same road, and when he saw the man, he passed by on the other side. 32 So too, a Levite, when he came to the place and saw him, passed by on the other side. 33 But a Samaritan, as he traveled, came where the man was; and when he saw him, he took pity on him. 34 He went to him and bandaged his wounds, pouring on oil and wine. Then he put the man on his own donkey, took him to an inn and took care of him. 35 The next day he took out two silver coins and gave them to the innkeeper. 'Look after him,' he said, 'and when I return, I will reimburse you for any extra expense you may have.'

36 Which of these three do you think was a neighbor to the man who fell into the hands of robbers?"

37 The expert in the law replied, "The one who had mercy on him." Jesus told him, "Go and do likewise."

Here, in Luke chapter 10, Jesus is telling the story of the Good Samaritan, a hated foreigner who acted with the compassion that is God. Jesus praised his actions towards the Jew left as dead in the ditch. He in turn criticized the Jewish religious hierarchy for putting religious rules and regulations before the man in need of help.

All religious movements at some time or other have disagreements within themselves, and ultimately they split into rival groups all claiming to hold the One Truth or to be the Only Genuine Inheritors of the Truth. For example, Islam is split in several ways, and the news from Iraq following the illegal invasion by Britain and America continually reminded us of two major opposing groups, the Sunnis and Shi'as.

But let us remember that Christianity has been split many more times than Islam: the great schism between the Eastern Orthodox Church and the Western Roman Catholic Church in 1054; and later still the Protestant and Catholic Divide in the 16th century, after the Frenchman John Calvin, the Scotsman John Knox, and the German Martin Luther ushered in Protestantism. There have been hundreds of subsequent splits into rival Protestant denominations that continue to this day; and it may be no different for those of us who are developing progressive Christianity and a new understanding of God and Jesus in a way that is more relevant than the creeds and doctrines and dogmas of a long dead age. We do so out of love for the message of Jesus and for the future of the Church that in this post-modern age is dying around us. It is our genuine attempt to save Jesus and to save the Church that doubtless we will cause further dissension and possibly suffer ex-communication as leaders of the progressive movement. That is the way of all religious movements.

But it was similar in the time of Jesus. According to Josephus, the Roman/Jewish historian writing 60 years after the first Easter, four major groups exercised the Jewish leadership at the time of Jesus. There were revolutionaries, such as the Zealots, and we should not forget, indeed we should ask why Jesus chose Simon the Zealot amongst his original twelve disciples. I wonder what that says about our picture of 'gentle Jesus meek and mild?' Further more, what does this suggest as far as those Christians are concerned who say that Christianity and politics should not mix?

The other three groups were the religious leaders – the Pharisees, the Essenes and the Sadducees. There were other small local religious movements that also came and went, but one of them, the Followers of the Way of Jesus of Nazareth not only came but continued after the execution of its leader and went on to become the Christian Church – in its many guises. And to this we are witnesses today.

In sermons and Bible readings we hear so much about Pharisees, Essenes and Sadducees, but what do we know about them; who were they and do they still exist? First of all, the Pharisees were not priests but they were a very important and powerful authority in the Law of Moses as seen within the written Hebrew Scriptures and as told from oral tradition. The Pharisees were the teachers and interpreters of the Law of Moses and they were especially popular amongst the pious poor. They considered their path to holiness was by separating themselves from those who did not follow their teaching, but it was a separation while living within the community. It was their painstaking observance of the Law of Moses that made them into rigid authoritarians.

Their religiousness got in the way of their humanity. This is what the Parable of the Good Samaritan is all about. Jesus seemed to have a go at them more than he did the other religious groups but, surprisingly, he does not include them in this parable of neglect and narrow-minded prejudice. However, the parable is an attack upon the Pharisees – after all, it is a story told by Jesus in direct response to the Pharisee who was trying to trick him with this question, "Who is my neighbor?" The Pharisees, like the Essenes and the Sadducees, believed that they were right, and every one else was wrong. Sadly, what was represented by the religious and political leadership of the Pharisees at the time of Jesus can still be seen in many religious movements today.

The Essenes are thought to have been descendants of an earlier split in the religious and priestly leadership of the Jerusalem Temple, losing out to the Sadducees some 200 years before the birth of Jesus. Like the Pharisees, the Essene

Community kept itself 'sanctified' by being detached from all who did not share their rigorous knowledge and understanding of their Hebrew faith. Like the Pharisees and the Sadducees, the Essenes believed that they were right and every one else was wrong. To highlight this point, the Essenes created small, out-of-the-way settlements throughout Judea, as well as the principal separated community of Qumran, about a mile inland from the northwestern shore of the Dead Sea in what we now call the Palestinian West Bank. It was in the caves above Qumran that the 900 parchments known to us as the Dead Sea Scrolls were found in 1947.

So, with the Pharisees being the lay leadership of the Jews, and the Essenes cut off from any possible contamination by the culture and politics of the time, who were the Sadducees? They were the aristocrats and the collaborators with the Roman occupiers and oppressors, enjoying the political power delegated to them by the Romans. But their major function was that of being the priests in the Jerusalem Temple. Like the Pharisees and the Essenes, the Sadducees believed that they were right and every one else was wrong. Theologically they were opposed to the Pharisees and politically opposed to the Jewish Zealot revolutionaries.

The basis of their holiness was in the Book of Leviticus chapters 17 – 26 concerning sacrifices and the holiness of blood; the wholesomeness of sexuality; regulations and punishments for breaking the rules; the sacredness of the priesthood; the festivals of the liturgical year; the Sabbatical Year and the Year of Jubilee. Unlike the Pharisees, there was a repudiation of oral tradition and all that was acceptable as the way of holy living was keeping the formal procedures, rules and regulations of the Book of Leviticus. In its victorious battle against Jewish revolutionaries, the Romans ruined the Jerusalem Temple in 70 C.E., and without the Temple the Sadducees and their Temple Cult vanished from history.

But the Parable of the Good Samaritan also talks about a Levite. 1000 years before Jesus, the military commander Joshua apportioned land to the tribes of Israel after they had conquered Canaan. However, the only tribe not to receive land was that of Levi. Instead, the Levites in return for performing religious and political duties in the Tabernacle and then in the Temple, were given some towns and received a tithe, a form of taxation applied to the landed tribes. Some of the obligations of the Levites included singing the Psalms in worship in the Temple, repairing and keeping the Temple building in good condition, and being responsible for guarding the Temple. From time to time the Levites also acted as both Judges and teachers of the Law of Moses.

Today Levites still have specific responsibilities within Orthodox Judaism. They continue to wash the hands of the priests before the Priestly Blessing. Orthodox Jews are obliged to take part in the Ceremony of the Redemption of their Firstborn, presenting them to be available for Divine service. However, all Levites are exempt as they are still seen as being set aside to serve God. Orthodox Jews, along with some extreme fundamentalist Christians, believe in and look forward to the day when the Temple will again be built in Jerusalem. It is the goal that when that day comes the wide-ranging role of the Levites will be taken up again.

So, what has all of this background to do with the Parable of the Good Samaritan? Jesus is attacking the Jewish religious leaders. He indirectly condemns the Pharisees, and by implication also the Essenes, while at the same time he directly attacks the Sadducees and the Levites for their exclusivity of life-style, looking down upon all who do not follow their interpretations of Judaism. Jesus condemns them all for allowing their traditional religion to get in the way of their humanity. Jesus is making the point – for then and for now: those who put rules and regulations, and creeds and doctrines, before the needs of others; those who put religion before humanity, have missed the point of what God is about.

Of course it is important for there to be mosques, temples, synagogues and churches as places of worship, fellowship and mutual support. They are to be places to remind adherents from whence they have come and why they exist. But they are not to be castles to protect people from the outside world by making them places of exclusivity, the attitude being "You can only become one of us when you become like us". Places of worship are to be the powerhouses in which all are accepted – places of inclusivity regardless of what people have been or what the people have become.

I am not in the least bothered by who you are or by what you might have been; by the color of your skin or by your gender or sexual orientation; by your marital status or otherwise; by your age or by your religion or lack of religion; by your understanding and experience of God. All that I am bothered about is the extent to which we accept one another with the unconditional, sacrificial and compassionate love that is God, so fully demonstrated to us in the life of Jesus of Nazareth. And that, as I understand the Parable of the Good Samaritan, is the way in which Jesus lived, and the example of how we are all called to live.

It is the only way forward in a world broken by power, money, greed and poverty; broken by the culture of "I am; I want; I must have, and I must have it now". Jesus asked the Pharisee,

36 "Which of these three do you think was a neighbor to the man who fell into the hands of robbers?" 37 The expert in the law replied, "The one who had mercy on him." Jesus told him, "Go and do likewise."

Luke 12: 13 – 21
The Parable of the rich fool

13 Someone in the crowd said, to him, "Teacher, tell my

brother to divide the inheritance with me." 14 Jesus replied, "Man, who appointed me a judge or an arbiter between you?" 15 Then he said, to them, "Watch out! Be on your guard against all kinds of greed; a man's life does not consist in the abundance of his possessions." 16 And he told them this parable: "The ground of a certain rich man produced a good crop. 17 He thought to himself, 'What shall I do? I have no place to store my crops.' 18 Then he said, "This is what I'll do. I will tear down my barns and build bigger ones, and there I will store all my grain and my goods. 19 And I'll say to myself, 'You have plenty of good things laid up for many years. Take life easy; eat, drink and be merry.' 20 But God said, to him, 'You fool! This very night your life will be demanded from you. Then who will get what you have prepared for yourself?' 21 This is how it will be with anyone who stores up things for himself but is not rich toward God."

Here we have the story of the younger brother who challenges the Mosaic Law of Inheritance and the parable about the rich man who places his future in the construction of barns to hold his increasing wealth. It is in the rich fool's storing up of everything for himself and using his wealth to have a good time rather than in using his wealth in the service of others, that Luke says he is 'poor in the sight of God.'

Wealth is not wrong in itself. The problem exists in how we gained and how we use our wealth. I am reminded of one of my working visits to post-Communist Eastern Europe. I was discussing with a local entrepreneur who, by then was a US dollar multi millionaire. He said, "I will not tell you how I made my first million but happy to tell you how I made my second!" If it has come from exploitation of the poor, or if we use it selfishly, for us alone, then we are poor in relation to the purposes of Perfect Love. But we are rich if we use our wealth, no matter if it is millions of dollars or pounds, or dozens of pennies in the support of those who have far less than we do. Wealth in the Kingdom of Perfect Love is not about how much we have in the bank but it is about how we use it for the common good.

Here in this parable of the rich fool Luke twice refers to the Gospel of Thomas. These are the 64th and the 72nd sayings of Jesus when he answers a man in the crowd who wants him to give a ruling because his brother is apparently withholding some inheritance from their father. I wonder if this younger brother is asking for half the amount left to the two sons by their father? If so, he is asking too much because the Book of Deuteronomy chapter 21 says that the elder brother should have a double portion of any inheritance. It was the Law of Moses.

On the surface, it doesn't seem fair to me, but with the double portion came double responsibility. It was for the elder son to take care of the surviving mother or mothers and the family after the father had died, and for that the elder son was given the double portion of the inheritance. Therefore the inheritance was split into three, with two-thirds going to the elder and one third to the younger. However, during the time of the patriarchs, the inheritance Law of Moses was modified so that the eldest son could either be disinherited or could be given the whole of the inheritance by the father.

This accommodation of the need to change remains the way of the world and the way of the Church; only usually it takes longer in the Church to bring about any change! You will recall that the unchangeable 'tablet of stone' attitude was the holiness code of the Pharisees, the Sadducees and the Essenes, and rejected and discredited by Jesus. Although some fundamentalist Christians today treat the Bible as a textbook with rules and regulations applicable to all times and in all places, in my understanding and experience, the Hebrew and Christian Scriptures must be regularly changed and adapted as life changes and develops because the Scriptures are a guidebook and not a rulebook for our journey and pilgrimage of faith.

That is why having a woman as an ordained member of the clergy was considered to be unbiblical 50 years ago but is now commonplace in mainline Protestant churches. One day it will be acceptable in the Catholic and Orthodox Churches as well! When my wife and I were in Canada on holiday in mid-2007 there was an ordination service of 'Catholic' women priests into the Open Episcopal Church. Needless to say these women priests are not recognized by the Vatican but they are recognized in their local Open Episcopal Catholic communities.

And homosexuality has been condemned by the Churches for two millennia, and still is condemned in many churches today. But once certain questions have been asked, for example, "Can a homosexual be a Christian?" and "Can practicing homosexuals be members of the clergy?" then the outcome is inevitable. Bishop Gene Robinson in the Episcopal Church of America and Jeffrey John, Dean of St Albans Cathedral in Hertfordshire, U.K. have changed this situation for the whole Church; and one day monogamous homosexuality will be widely accepted as a true and genuine expression of the Perfect Love that is God, and clergy will be fully accepted in the ordained ministry, regardless of their gender or sexual orientation. As Bishop Jack Spong says, "Once the question is asked the outcome is inevitable. The only question that is left is how long can the Church resist the change?"

Now, back to the Parable of the rich fool. It is Luke alone amongst the Canonical Gospels who has this story of the younger brother who should have known the Mosaic Laws of inheritance. It seems to me that the younger brother had gone to Rabbi Jesus to ask for an interpretation of the Mosaic Law that could be used by him when he returned to his elder brother to say, "Give me a greater share of the inheritance because Rabbi Jesus says so."

This encounter, at least for me, is further evidence as to why I think that Jesus was a Pharisee at the beginning of his ministry but, by now in the order in which Luke tells the story, Jesus was moving away from the Pharisaic intransigence and holiness of separation. Although the role of the Pharisee was one of teacher and interpreter of the Laws of Moses, Jesus did not get involved in this dispute between the brothers. He simply asked, "Who gave me the right to settle arguments between you and your brother?" Here, as I interpret Luke the Outsider, Jesus has moved on from the rules and regulations of the Pharisees to a new understanding and experience of God in which compassion and common sense were more important than the traditionalism of "this is the way we have always done things around here."

Then comes the parable, told not just to this young brother but also to the entire crowd. It is a message that would have been well received by the poor who seemed often to be the largest part of any crowd that came to Jesus. It is a message that is particularly important to Luke in which the Kingdom of God will reverse the norms of society so that the rich will be laid low and the poor will be exalted. Isn't this also the message of Mary's Song, the Magnificat, in Luke chapter 1:46-55?

As, mentioned earlier, if Goulder is correct then Luke wrote the story of the barns and stores of grain and other goods for use at the time of the Jewish Festival of Shavuot celebrated seven weeks after Pentecost. This makes sense to me, as Shavuot celebrates the end of the barley harvest and the start of the wheat harvest! This story, put into the mouth of Jesus, was Luke's warning to the people to take care with how they approached the festival of Shavuot and the blessings of harvest, so that these blessings were not used just for themselves but in the service of others, Jew and Gentile alike.

Luke 12: 49 – 56
Not peace but division

In a letter to *The Times* newspaper on 5th September 1919,

Admiral John Fisher wrote, "Never contradict. Never explain. Never apologize". He was wrong on all three counts! Contradiction, explanation and apologies are vital in any democracy, including in the Church. If we are to understand the strange 'un-Jesus like' statements in Luke chapter 12:49 to 56, then we also need to read what is on the line and between the lines and behind the lines!

This is one of those strange passages that at first looking seems to be completely out of character for Jesus. Here we have Jesus, the Prince of Peace, telling people that he has come, not to bring peace but to set fire to the earth. Equally Luke has Jesus reprimanding the people for they know how to tell the weather in advance, but they cannot read the obvious signs of the times of political and economic oppression at the hands of the Roman conquerors. Luke has brought these two passages together suggesting that Jesus was involved in these two stories at the same time, in the same place and with the same people. However, Matthew's Gospel has included both these passages but at different times: the passage about not bringing peace is in Matthew 10 and reading the signs of the times is in Matthew 16. This is nothing new, and there are many more examples when comparing the four Gospels included in the Christian scriptures. So who is right, Luke or Matthew?

It is essential that we remember that the Gospel writers were writing within the culture, environment, political and economic contexts and realities of their specific local followers. They were *not* writing when Jesus was alive and nor were they writing for you or me! As such these Gospels are hindsight interpretations of the life of Jesus set within a social commentary upon the communities that followed his way and teaching, thirty to sixty years after that first Easter. The Gospels are not God's word on Jesus but they are records of the community memories and experiences of Jesus. So how can we know if Jesus really said and did the things that the Gospel writers attribute to him? In all honesty we can't but there are additional sources that may help us to decide.

As the Gospel of Thomas was probably the first Gospel to have been written I tend to take the line: 'If the saying is in the Gospel of Thomas, it is probable that Jesus said it, or something very close to it.' So has Thomas any reference to these two sayings in Matthew and Luke concerning Jesus *not* bringing peace but division, and the failure of the people to read the signs of the time? Saying 9 of Thomas states, "Jesus said, I have cast a fire upon the world, and lo, I keep it until it burns up". And saying 16 of Thomas states:

Jesus said, "Perhaps some men think that I came to cast peace on the world; and they do not know that I came to cast division upon the earth, fire, sword, war. For five will be in a house; there will be three against two and two against three, the father against the son and the son against the father. And they will stand because they are single ones."

Now consider again Luke's chapter 12 version of the Thomas sayings 9 and 16:

49 "I have come to bring fire on the earth, and how I wish it were already kindled! 50 But I have a baptism to undergo, and how distressed I am until it is completed! 51 Do you think I came to bring peace on earth? No, I tell you, but division. 52 From now on there will be five in one family divided against each other, three against two and two against three. 53 They will be divided, father against son and son against father, mother against daughter and daughter against mother, mother-in-law against daughter-in-law and daughter-in-law against mother-in-law."

And Mathew's version is in chapter 10:34 – 36:

34 "Do not suppose that I have come to bring peace to the earth. I did not come to bring peace, but a sword. 35 For I have come to turn a man against his father, a daughter against her mother, a daughter-in-law against her mother-in-law. 36 A man's enemies will be the members of his own household."

So Luke has Jesus bringing fire to the earth and Matthew has Jesus bringing a sword.

But these are essentially the same stories and both Matthew and Luke in all probability have taken them from Thomas. Therefore I am happy to accept that Jesus did indeed talk about bringing fire and sword to earth rather than peace. But what on earth did the Prince of Peace – the one who broke down barriers that divided, the one who sought to bring unity – what did Jesus mean when he said these things? Surely Jesus was *not* saying that he was the Cosmic Destroyer!

As I read the Gospel stories I see Jesus moving increasingly away from his early Rabbinic teachings, becoming the pragmatist – freeing himself of tradition and dogma and responding to the needs of others and to the need for change. Here was Jesus, the non-violent, civil disobedient leader of a ragtag group of women and men. Time and again the Gospel stories show us that he was prepared to adapt and to develop to meet the changing demands both in society and in the lives of his followers.

I interpret these two stories, the bringing of division, and the reading of the signs of the times, as Jesus reflecting upon the social and political realities in his time. Jesus was warning that division will be the natural outcome of following him and his teaching, but he had not come specifically to bring division. Here was Jesus living within an occupied country and he was asking his followers to make the choice: "Follow the revelation of the universal and inclusive Yahweh God, no longer just for the Jews but for all people; or continue to follow the outmoded exclusive

Yahweh God of traditional Judaism; or follow the Roman Caesar God – you cannot follow more than one master."

It was a stark choice, and one that set Jesus on a clear collision course both with the Jewish political and religious leadership and with Rome. Jesus was preparing those of his followers who were ready to make the choice for the universal and inclusive Yahweh God: "Follow my way of non-violent civil disobedience and you *may* find the fire and the sword of the Temple and of Rome descending upon you. But, take up arms against Rome and you will surely find the fire and sword of Caesar descending upon you."

And again, the context in which Matthew and Luke wrote their respective Gospels is important. They were writing in the aftermath of the horrendous Jewish revolt against Rome that resulted in the destruction of the Jerusalem Temple and the mass suicide of Jewish fighters at Masada. The Zealots and the Sadducees had not heeded the warning of Jesus.

So I interpret these passages in both Matthew and Luke concerning fire and the sword, rather than peace, as both Gospel writers warning their own followers that they are to be careful when facing up to the reality of Roman occupation. What happened to Jesus at the hands of Rome could also happen to them. Once again we can see in Matthew's Gospel in particular, a considerable shift in loyalty as Matthew the Jew distanced his Jewish and Gentile community from the Jews who rejected the ways of Jesus, and especially from the Sadducees who had supported the revolt against Rome. It is important to remember that, at the same time, Matthew sought favor with the new regime in Rome.

Remember, also, at the moment of the death of Jesus, it is Matthew's Gospel alone that has the Roman soldier – rather than a Jew – first to recognize Jesus as God's Son. This is significant because Matthew's community was living in Caesarea Maritima where, according to the first century historian Josephus, a Roman massacre of Jews in 67 C.E. fuelled the Roman War that had commenced only a short time before.

As also noted earlier, Matthew's Gospel is the most Jewish in nature and its anti-Semitism has given rise to the most appalling 'Christian' persecution of Jews down the past two millennia, culminating in the extermination camps of the likes of Auschwitz-Birkenau and Treblinka, and the concentration camps such as Dachau and Belsen and Buchenwald.

But now we turn to the second part of this passage where Jesus reprimands all who were listening to him because they could not discern the signs of the times. In Luke 12:54 – 56 we read:

> 54 Jesus said, to the crowd: "When you see a cloud rising in the west, immediately you say, 'It's going to rain,' and it does. 55 And when the south wind blows, you say, 'It's going to be hot,' and it is. 56 Hypocrites! You know how to interpret the appearance of the earth and the sky. How is it that you don't know how to interpret this present time?"

Has Thomas anything to say about this story? Partly, yes, but with a slightly different emphasis. The Gospel of Thomas saying 4 states:

> Jesus said, "Know what is before your face, and what is hidden from you will be revealed to you; for there is nothing hidden which will not be manifest."

As I understand this Thomas saying, Jesus was giving a clear warning to his followers to know what they were getting into by choosing the universal and inclusive Yahweh and not Caesar as God. It was a further warning to those of his followers who were moving towards armed insurrection against Rome. To Jesus the realist, the result of taking on Rome with weapons of war rather than with the power of civil disobedient Love would be the fire and the sword of Rome. And what had applied while Jesus was making these statements still applied while Matthew and Luke were writing their Gospels fifty or so years later.

I am convinced that is why both Matthew and Luke, writing *after* the disastrous rebellion, include these sayings, and why Mark, writing before the rebellion and without the Gospel of Thomas open in front of him, does not include them.

But do these two Jesus statements in Luke chapter 12 have anything to say to us today? We all need to make up our own minds on this, but to me, the implication of Jesus warning his followers is that to follow His way will lead to division within some families and to conflict with the ruling powers. I guess that most of us have members of our families or friends who disagree with us about our understanding and interpretation of the Bible, and of Jesus and of God. Let me reassure you that there is nothing new in this – Jesus was warning about this two thousand years ago! To follow the ways of Jesus will sometimes, in some families, result in doubt and incredulity or 'behind the back' criticism or, sadly, even in open conflict. If this is your situation be assured that you are not alone!

And further, to take on the ruling powers – government, for example – may sometimes result in a process that begins with ignoring, and if you persist will lead to open criticism stating that you are wrong; and if you continue in your challenge then comes the marginalizing and ultimately the character assassination. This is how the Temple authorities treated Jesus.

This is how the British Government treated its own scientist and arms expert Dr David Kelly who had been outspoken about intelligence being exaggerated to make the case for the invasion of Iraq. The response of the Government to Kelly's opposition was the process of ignoring, then criticizing, then marginalizing and then finally of character assassination. It resulted in Dr Kelly's suicide on 22nd July 2003. But there is nothing new in this process. Jesus understood all too clearly the dangers of taking on the ruling economic and religious and political powers. It resulted in his execution on Calvary's Cross, not because some claimed that he was the Son of God but because the Roman authorities accused him of being King of the Jews.

As for reading the signs of the times? It is vital for us to keep up to date with what is happening in our world. How can we challenge abuse of power unless we have the information? Central and local government can abuse their powers, and when they do so, they need to be challenged. It can be cell/mobile telephone companies attempting to erect telephone masts or the large supermarket chains wanting to build in the midst of where people live and then abusing democratically elected councils by threatening to financially cripple local government should planning decisions go against the company concerned. If they abuse their powers they need to be challenged.

It can be the leadership of our churches wherever Perfect Love is abused or people are discriminated against owing to bigotry and narrow-minded vindictiveness. If Church leadership abuses its powers it needs to be challenged.

And in 2007, when we in Britain were celebrating the bi-centenary of the end of the transatlantic slave trade, Sir Philip Green's Arcadia company – with its clothing stores Top Shop, Top Man, Burton, Dorothy Perkins and Miss Selfridge – was challenged by many individuals and organizations. Why? Because Asian workers, recruited to work in the factories of Mauritius that are used by Arcadia, were allegedly required to work 12-hour days, 6 days a week for a maximum 40 pence an hour, less than half the average wage in Mauritius. Does this not amount to slave labor in the factories of Mauritius used to produce the garments for these stores? How can the Followers of Jesus keep silent in the face of such as this?

Those involved in the civil disobedience at the 2007 Climate Camp at London Heathrow Airport – as long as the protest remained non-violent – were acting in the dignified tradition of non-violent civil disobedience of Jesus, Ghandi and Dr Martin Luther King. As Jonathan Bartley put it on BBC Radio 4's 'Thought for the Day' on the Thursday morning during the week-long Airport protest, "Those who are today's civil disobedient often become tomorrow's saviors."

There are two pertinent statements attributed to the 18th century Irish political philosopher, politician and statesman, Edmund Burke: first, 'All that is necessary for evil to triumph is for good men to do nothing,' and second, 'nothing is so fatal to religion as indifference.' Christian faith that does not result in political action is no more than a puff of air. Jesus understood, all too clearly, the need to read the signs of the times and then to make the choice between keeping silent or speaking out and having to face the consequences.

As followers of the Way of Jesus of Nazareth, we must be informed and we must act. We cannot be indifferent to the injustices in this world. The Eternal Spirit fully manifested in Jesus calls each one of us to make a choice between serving God and serving and supporting the unjust and exploitative powers of this age, with all their respective rewards and consequences. That same Eternal Spirit challenges us to make our decisions to be on the side of the poor and the exploited, but we should know that to make this choice opens ourselves to the fire and the sword; to division within families and between friends; sometimes with the political and ecclesiastic powers. To follow the Way of Jesus is no easy option. From time to time it will cost us dearly. But what other choice do we really have if we want to follow Jesus and to live God's Kingdom here and now?

Luke 14:1-14
Jesus at a Pharisee's House

1 One Sabbath, when Jesus went to eat in the house of a

prominent Pharisee, he was being carefully watched. 2 There in front of him was a man suffering from dropsy. 3 Jesus asked the Pharisees and experts in the Law, "Is it Lawful to heal on the Sabbath or not?" 4 But they remained silent. So taking hold of the man, he healed him and sent him away.

5 Then he asked them, "If one of you has a son or an ox that falls into a well on the Sabbath day, will you not immediately pull him out?" 6 And they had nothing to say.

7 When he noticed how the guests picked the places of honor at the table, he told them this parable: 8 "When someone invites you to a wedding feast, do not take the place of honor, for a person more distinguished than you may have been invited. 9 If so, the host who invited both of you will come and say to you, 'Give this man your seat.' Then, humiliated, you will have to take the least important place. 10 But when you are invited, take the lowest place, so that when your host comes, he will say to you, 'Friend, move up to a better place.' Then you will be honored in the presence of all your fellow guests. 11 For everyone who exalts himself will be humbled, and he who humbles himself will be exalted."

12 Then Jesus said to his host, "When you give a luncheon or dinner, do not invite your friends, your brothers or relatives, or your rich neighbors; if you do, they may invite you back and so you will be repaid. 13 But when you give a banquet, invite the poor, the crippled, the lame, the blind, 14 and you will be blessed. Although they cannot repay you, you will be repaid at the resurrection of the righteous."

I ask two questions, 'Why was Jesus invited to the home of a prominent Pharisee for yet another meal? And why were other Pharisees and teachers of the Law of Moses continuing to carefully watch Jesus?' Has it now reached a point where the Pharisees are so suspicious of Jesus, especially if he had originally been a Pharisee himself, that they are watching his every move before deciding how to condemn him and exclude him? Remember the process of alienation by the powers and authorities: ignoring, open criticism, marginalizing and ultimately the character or actual assassination.

Think back at how Jesus and his disciples had already challenged the traditions and legalism of the Sabbath. From my reading of the Gospel stories, although Jesus did certain things that the Law of Moses required of him, like tithing to the Levites; telling the healed leper to go to the priest to give a gift in thanks, as commanded by Moses; keeping the custom of the Passover meal etc. Jesus never told anyone to keep the Sabbath as the day of rest and prayer as strictly as laid down in the 10 Commandments. Indeed, Jesus seemed to have developed a very open-minded and generous approach to the Sabbath, putting compassion and personal need ahead of the strict observance of the command not to work on the Sabbath.

In Luke chapter 4, as soon as the ministry of Jesus began, his own people in Nazareth rejected him. Jesus then went to Capernaum and, on the Sabbath, taught the people in the synagogue. This could have been a building or just someone's home, but whatever, it was the Jewish meeting place and centre of community life. But when a man with an evil spirit called out, Jesus did not say, "I know I can help you, but I can't do it until sundown because I cannot work on the Sabbath – come back later if you want my help." According to Luke, Jesus had compassion and immediately responded to the needs of this man and healed him there and then. This was illegal under the Law of Moses.

Do not be confused as to when Sabbath occurs. Sabbath is from sunset on Friday until sunset on Saturday, during which time no work is undertaken. It is a day of rest and a day set aside for worship. It is the fourth of the Ten Commandments of Moses and so important as a sign of the Covenant that Israel claimed Yahweh God had made with it that, according to Exodus chapter 31, anyone breaking the Sabbath was to be put to death. But under Roman occupation, no Jew had the right to execute another even for working on the Sabbath. The response of the people to what Jesus had done in the synagogue was amazement. But the response of the synagogue leaders to Jesus on this first occasion of breaking the Sabbath Law was public silence. No doubt there was private concern but publicly, what Jesus has done was ignored.

According to Luke's chapter 4 account of that Sabbath day, Jesus had not yet finished breaking the Sabbath Law. He went over to Simon Peter's house where he found Simon's mother-in-Law sick with fever; and before the sunset, so it was still Sabbath, Jesus had compassion and healed her. People's needs were more important than keeping the Sabbath Law, even though the breaking of that Law was a religious capital offence.

In Luke chapter 4 the news of what Jesus is doing, on and off the Sabbath, spreads far and wide, so that when we get to Luke chapter 5 Pharisees and the experts in the Law of Moses come to see for themselves from throughout Galilee, Judea and even as far as Jerusalem. Some may have been truly interested in finding out about this new phenomenon, whilst others may have been there to gather evidence with which they could later condemn Jesus.

When Jesus not only healed but also forgave the sin of a crippled man, the cat was well and truly set amongst the pigeons and Jesus and the Pharisees and the experts in the Law were now on a collision course. The time for ignoring Jesus was over. Now came the open criticism. The Pharisees and experts in the Law began arguing and saying, "Jesus is deluded. He thinks that he is God but only God can forgive sins." Everyone was amazed and praised God, everyone except some of the Pharisees and experts in the Law. The ignoring and the open criticism now began to give way to marginalizing.

At first the Pharisees and teachers of the Law tried to undermine Jesus, including amongst his disciples. They went to the disciples while Jesus and they were eating with Matthew the tax collector and others considered to be sinners. And here was Jesus, the one who not only healed but now forgave sins, ceasing to be holy in the eyes of the Pharisees: "How can a holy man eat with those whom we consider to be sinners?" If Jesus had begun his ministry as a Pharisee then he could no longer be one of them because their holiness was in keeping themselves separate from all who were considered to be sinners.

Jesus responded to them simply by saying, "I didn't come to invite good people [like you] to turn to God. I came to invite sinners." Here was the action of a fully human Jesus giving an 'in your face' response to the Pharisees. It was a direct attack upon the holiness of separation that was the keystone of Pharisaic way of life. Jesus was attacking the Pharisees by saying that God accepted those whom the Pharisees rejected.

Then in chapter 6, Luke has Jesus being questioned by the Pharisees about the Sabbath. Jesus and his disciples had been walking through the wheat field and, in their hunger, picked the wheat, rubbed the husks off with their hands and ate the grain. This was another direct attack upon the Pharisees and the way in which they excluded any such activity – considered to be work on the Sabbath. Luke has Jesus conclude this episode with the clear statement, "The Son of Man is Lord over the Sabbath." This is red rag to a bull, and the criticism of Jesus now comes increasingly out into the open. Chapter 6 continues again in a synagogue on the Sabbath, and again Jesus heals a man with a crippled hand.

Luke has the Pharisees and teachers of the Law of Moses present so that they could be ready to accuse Jesus of doing something wrong should he heal anyone that day and they get what they have come to see. Luke has this incident end with the Pharisees and teachers of the Law furious and beginning to plot how they can get rid of him. This is followed in chapter 8 by Simon the Pharisee inviting Jesus to a meal in order to test him.

But Luke drops the Pharisees from his Gospel from here until they reappear in the last section of chapter 11. Another unnamed Pharisee invites Jesus to a meal but is astonished that Jesus does not go through the required purification process before he eats. Here Jesus really gets tough with the Pharisees and the teachers of the Law who are present, calling them fools and those who are in for trouble because they cheat others and want places of honor at meal tables and in public places. A teacher of the Law tries to defend himself but Jesus tells them some more home truths. At the end of this Luke has the Pharisees wanting to get even with Jesus. They want him publicly to say things about other people, presumably the other rulers in the Temple, King Herod in the Palace, and Pilate, Caesar and the Roman occupation.

There is another brief respite from the Pharisees, until chapter 13 when Jesus was again in the synagogue on the Sabbath and he healed a woman who had been crippled for eighteen years. The leader of the synagogue was angry because there were six days for this kind of thing, and the Sabbath was no time for healing work to be undertaken. The response of Jesus shamed those whom Luke now, for the first time, calls 'the enemies of Jesus.' The marginalizing of Jesus continued when some Pharisees went to him to tell that Herod wanted to kill him. Now these may have been helpful Pharisees, not part of those who wanted to destroy Jesus, so they were giving him a friendly warning to enable him to escape by leaving the territory governed by Herod. On the other hand this may have been just another attempt at marginalizing by trying to encourage Jesus to leave, not only Herod's territory but the area of their own influence and authority.

And here in Luke chapter 14 we again see Jesus invited to a meal with a Pharisee on the Sabbath. Present again were other Pharisees and teachers of the Law, and all were watching to gather further evidence for them to character assassinate Jesus in the public eye. It is here that we find a man suffering from dropsy and Jesus heals him.

Religious Jews at the time of Jesus would have upheld certain prohibitions on the Sabbath. In Exodus chapter 16:23, it is stated that God told the people to bake and prepare food before the Sabbath and eat only that previously prepared food during Sabbath. Nothing could be done that was associated with the baking of bread. That included the ploughing of fields, the sifting of the grain, separating the wheat from the chaff and the firing of ovens to bake the bread. This was extended to all farm work and household cooking. Starting a fire on which to cook was also considered to be work, and unless there was a serious threat to human life, if a fire broke out by accident they were not allowed to put out the fire, even though the house or building would be burned to the ground.

Working on the Sabbath also excluded any work on garments, including as much as putting in two stitches or the intentional tearing of cloth or the washing and dyeing of wool. Any activities involving leatherwork or building work were prohibited. All this left very little that God-fearing Jews were allowed to do on the Sabbath apart from rest, worship and pray.

In response to the criticism of the Pharisees, Luke continued to hit home his ongoing message: Jesus turns the tables on the Pharisees and the teachers of the Law of Moses and asks them who wouldn't save son or oxen if either fell into a well on the Sabbath? Here is the continuing attack upon the implementation of the Law of Moses, the leaders preaching one thing and yet, when push comes to shove, doing the exact opposite. No wonder Jesus often called the Pharisees 'hypocrites.' But what a warning that remains for us today – do we say one thing in public and yet do the opposite in private? Could Jesus condemn us in the same way?

But consider again the dinner at the beginning of chapter 14. All the important guests tried to take the best seats. Only Luke has this story. And three chapters before, Luke also has Jesus condemn the teachers of the Law of Moses for honoring themselves and forgetting to help those in need. Even before that, in chapter 9, it was not only a Pharisaic problem because the disciples of Jesus also argued about who was the greatest amongst them. And the response of Jesus on that occasion was, "Which ever one is the most humble is the greatest." And yet, even in chapter 22 the disciples of Jesus have still not got the message. They argue again at the Last Supper as to who is the greatest amongst them. And the response of Jesus that time was, "He who is greatest is to be servant of all."

So, here is Luke turning the ways of the world the right way up: invite and honor those who cannot return the compliment, the poor and outcast, rather than invite the rich and famous to make you feel important; do not preach one thing and practice another; the one who is greatest of all is the servant of all. As Jesus said, "If you humble yourself, you will be honored." The more I read Luke's Gospel the more I see Jesus as the non-violent political activist and not the 'gentle Jesus meek and mild' who never upset any body by some 'wishy-washy', 'touchy feely,' ineffectual life-style.

Jesus was not creating a fantasy world, or some unreachable utopia, but his wisdom and example are the very things that will change us and change this world for the better. To live the Ways of Jesus will make the self-satisfied feel distressed and yet will give hope and support to the poor and exploited so that they may receive a fair share of all the good things of Creation. The wisdom of Jesus is worth living for. It was also the wisdom that Jesus found worth dying for.

Luke 14:25–33
The Cost of Being a Disciple

25 Large crowds were traveling with Jesus, and turning to them he said, 26 "If anyone comes to me and does not hate his

father and mother, his wife and children, his brothers and sisters—yes, even his own life—he cannot be my disciple. 27 And anyone who does not carry his cross and follow me cannot be my disciple. 28 Suppose one of you wants to build a tower. Will he not first sit down and estimate the cost to see if he has enough money to complete it? 29 For if he lays the foundation and is not able to finish it, everyone who sees it will ridicule him, 30 saying, 'This fellow began to build and was not able to finish.' 31 Or suppose a king is about to go to war against another king. Will he not first sit down and consider whether he is able with ten thousand men to oppose the one coming against him with twenty thousand? 32 If he is not able, he will send a delegation while the other is still a long way off and will ask for terms of peace. 33 In the same way, any of you who does not give up everything he has cannot be my disciple."

I have a policy that I will not speak harshly about other religious groups. However, at this moment I break that rule because in the context of this reading concerning the cost of discipleship, there are some so-called exclusive Christian groups who use our text in Luke 14:25–33 as both an encouragement to and a requirement of converts. It goes something like this: "When you become a member of our Church, and remember that we are the only Church that has discovered the keys to Heaven, then, if they will not come with you, you will have to leave behind your father and mother, your wife and children, your brothers and sisters—yes, even your own life and all that you own. And then you will become what we tell you to be. Without such abandonment you cannot be a disciple of the only true and living Church of Jesus."

These often are sects that are exclusive in their membership and ruled as an undemocratic one-man [and it usually is] autocracy. One such sect has some ninety-eight congregations in the UK, and a major stronghold of the fifteen thousand members is in the south east of England. Members follow the strict requirements of the Elders' interpretations of the Bible. The followers of this religious group are protected from the world outside because it is considered to be evil. The education of their children is provided within a network of its forty-three schools. Their adult men work for the companies owned by the sect. The adult women, who can be seen in the supermarkets and town centre shops in their obligatory blue or white headscarves, marry young and remain at home to raise their many children. They are not allowed to drink alcohol, smoke, listen to the radio, read newspapers, possess a mobile/cell phone, watch television, take part in sport, go on to a university education, or eat with those considered to be 'unclean.'

Although under the current leadership the rules are being slightly relaxed, any member who is ostracized or voluntarily leaves must usually accept that, as far as the family members who remain in the sect are concerned, the leaver is dead. No further contact is allowed between family members who remain in and those who are outside the sect. And any family member who transgresses the rules and requirements is 'shut up': the term for being ostracized from the Fellowship. This can be applied to whole families if any member should dare to break the rules.

I am harsh in my attitudes towards the life-style of such sects because surely this is not what Luke meant when he quoted Matthew's Gospel chapter 10:37-38 concerning the warnings of the cost of discipleship: "Anyone who loves his father or mother more than me is not worthy of me; anyone who loves his son or daughter more than me is not worthy of me; and anyone who does not take his cross and follow me is not worthy of me;" and surely this is not what Luke meant when he quoted the 56th saying of Jesus recorded in the earlier Gospel of Thomas where Jesus said, "He who will not hate his father or his mother cannot be my disciple. And he who will not hate his brothers and his sisters, and carry his cross as I have, will not become worthy of me."

So what was Luke, along with Thomas and Matthew, trying to communicate concerning this warning of Jesus and the cost of being one of his disciples? In my understanding, the Gospel writers were not saying that Jesus required families to be split if any one wanted to be a disciple of Jesus. Nor were they saying that the Jesus Movement was to be exclusive and restricted to those who abandoned family ties and economic security.

As I consider Luke 14:25-33 within the whole picture of the Gospel records of the life of Jesus, what I see are further examples of the realism of Jesus that knew that to follow him would inevitably cost the individual. This was based upon the personal experience of Jesus who was, even in the early part of his ministry, rejected by friends and family alike. When I mention this to people, sometimes there is a shocked amazement that the 'holy family', often presented to us as the archetypal family, actually thought that Jesus was mad and they tried to pull him back from his mission and ministry. The evidence for me saying this is in Mark chapter 3:20-21 where we read, '20 Then Jesus entered a house, and again a crowd gathered, so that he and his disciples were not even able to eat. 21 When his family heard about this, they went to take charge of him, for they said, "He is out of his mind."'"

Luke does not include Mark's account of this early family rift, but later, in Luke chapter 8 there is the stand off between Jesus and his mother and brothers. Luke tells it in a gentle manner:

19 Now Jesus' mother and brothers came to see him, but they were not able to get near him because of the crowd. 20 Someone told him, "Your mother and brothers are standing outside, wanting to see you." 21 He replied, "My mother and brothers are those who hear God's word and put it into practice."

The implications here are that, at this time, his mother and brothers were still not following him or his teaching, and that they had rejected what he was doing and, in turn, had been rejected by him. There are similar gentle accounts of this incident in Thomas, saying 96, and in Matthew chapter 12:46-50, and in Mark chapter 3:31-35. However, in Mark chapter 6:4 there is an indication that the situation had deteriorated further between Jesus and his family: 4 Jesus said, to them, "Only in his hometown, among his relatives and in his own house is a prophet without honor."

In Luke 14:25-33 there is an echo of the situation in Luke chapter 12 where Jesus was talking about bringing sword and fire to the earth. It was not the mission of Jesus to divide but it was the realism of Jesus that knew to follow his alternative wisdom and life style would inevitably divide people. So Luke repeats the warnings of Jesus that to follow him will be costly. Luke also has Jesus warning the people to think carefully before committing to follow his ways:

> 28 Suppose one of you wants to build a tower. Will he not first sit down and estimate the cost to see if he has enough money to complete it? 29 For if he lays the foundation and is not able to finish it, everyone who sees it will ridicule him, 30 saying, 'This fellow began to build and was not able to finish.' 31 Or suppose a king is about to go to war against another king. Will he not first sit down and consider whether he is able with ten thousand men to oppose the one coming against him with twenty thousand?

Discipleship costs, but why do the Matthew and Luke accounts of the cost of discipleship differ so much? Matthew says it all in two verses, so why does Luke, less than a decade later, feel the need to expand these two common verses into a passage that is eight verses long, adding the details about building the tower and the king gathering an inferior army for battle? Perhaps Luke uses contemporary examples to demonstrate that it is best to be well prepared for any eventuality so that when the going gets tough, we are prepared and able to hang in there?

Perhaps there was experience in the geographic area of Luke's community of someone having started but who never completed the building of a tower? But that's something for further research! Perhaps Luke, in the years immediately following the defeat of the Jews by Rome, is reminding his readers that discipleship is not about going out to cause confrontation and dissension as a mark or proof of that discipleship, especially when the opposition is stronger? Perhaps Luke is saying that discipleship is not about encouraging persecution as though it is the equivalent of getting stripes of promotion on the military shirt?

But Luke *is* saying that following the wisdom and ways of Jesus will result, sometimes, in our being rejected for the stand that we take. It should be no surprise when we are ridiculed or made fun of by those who fail to comprehend the message and example of Jesus being lived out in our lives. Genuine discipleship costs and some know just what that means within families and amongst friends and colleagues.

And finally, why does Luke add verse 33 to this section concerning giving all possessions away to be the follower of Jesus? Remember that Luke also wrote the Book of Acts, chronicling the events in the early churches, starting from Jerusalem and then spreading throughout the Roman Empire. One of the things that the Followers of the Way of Jesus did in the early churches was to give everything to the common cause for the common good. So Luke may have added v33 specifically to encourage his readers to give everything they owned to the local community of the Followers of the Way of Jesus so that all, regardless of the Roman occupation, could live in spiritual liberty, economic equality and social fraternity.

Now that's not only a motto for Christians to conjure with but is it how we should live God's Kingdom here and now? I do not believe the pattern for the first century is necessarily the pattern for the twenty-first century. However, the principle still applies – it is the principle of the generosity of love in action.

Luke 15: 1 – 10
One sheep – one coin

[1]Now the tax collectors and "sinners" were all gathering around to hear him. [2]But the Pharisees and the teachers of the law muttered, "This man welcomes sinners and eats with them."

[3]Then Jesus told them this parable: [4]"Suppose one of you has a hundred sheep and loses one of them. Does he not leave the ninety-nine in the open country and go after the lost sheep until he finds it? [5]And when he finds it, he joyfully puts it on his shoulders [6]and goes home. Then he calls his friends and neighbors together and says, 'Rejoice with me; I have found my lost sheep.' [7]I tell you that in the same way there will be more rejoicing in heaven over one sinner who repents than over ninety-nine righteous persons who do not need to repent.

The Parable of the Lost Coin

[8]"Or suppose a woman has ten silver coins and loses one. Does she not light a lamp, sweep the house and search carefully until she finds it? [9]And when she finds it, she calls her friends and neighbors together and says, 'Rejoice with me; I have found my lost coin.' [10]In the same way, I tell you, there is rejoicing in the presence of the angels of God over one sinner who repents."

Here we have another story of a shepherd! And once again, the context of the story is that the tax collectors, those who were collaborators with the Roman oppressors, and other sinners were crowding in to listen to Jesus. However, the Pharisees and the teachers of the Law of Moses are present once again, listening, watching, waiting, all the while gathering evidence for their final attempt to destroy the work of Jesus by destroying Jesus himself.

Reading the Gospel of Luke is like watching the cut and thrust of a Tom and Jerry cartoon! The Pharisees grumble about Jesus eating with tax collectors and sinners and so Jesus turns the tables on them again. Jesus tells the story of the shepherd who has a hundred sheep and one of them goes missing. In the Gospel of Thomas saying 104 reads:

Jesus said, "The kingdom is like a shepherd who had 100 sheep. One of them, the largest, lost his way. He left the 99 and sought the one until he found it. After he had toiled, he said, to the sheep, I love you more than the 99."

Thomas uses this story as an insight into the kingdom of God. However, Matthew and Luke take this story to demonstrate the on-going conflict between Jesus and the Pharisees and the teachers of the Law of Moses. But as often happens, Luke copies the earlier Gospel of Matthew and then adds his own comments. Here we have Luke adding v7 to the Matthew account of the lost sheep. Luke says that there is more happiness in heaven because one sinner turns to God than over 99 good people who don't need to. In other words, here is another attack upon the Pharisees and the teachers of the Law of Moses, these so-called spiritual leaders and experts, who considered themselves to be righteous but also unfairly judged the tax collectors and sinners to be beyond the love of God.

Luke shows Jesus once again to be someone who was not undermining Judaism but was one who was trying to reform it to encompass all people everywhere, without exception and without conditions. Luke has Jesus saying to the Pharisees and the teachers of the Law of Moses, "You think that you are righteous and chosen by God, so you don't need me. But because you will not accept the tax collectors and sinners, I will go to them because God's love is for them."

That was a radical message for then and remains a radical message for us today. God is the Spirit of Perfect Love that is within all and about all and beyond all, the imminent and the transcendent. And often we fail to see God coming to us day-by-day in those round about us, simply because we are not looking for God in those who are different to us. We also fail to see God in those whom we find unpleasant and in those who we would prefer not to meet and greet, and certainly in those with whom we would not want to eat. The message of Luke's Gospel, including the message of the lost sheep and the lost coin, is that God's love is for everyone regardless of what we think! And the way we live should reflect the transforming Gospel imperative: "The Perfect Love that is God, loves perfectly all those who are imperfect.

Luke 16:19-31
The Rich Man and Lazarus

19 There was a rich man who was dressed in purple and fine linen and lived in luxury every day. 20 At his gate was laid a beggar named Lazarus, covered with sores 21 and longing to eat what fell from the rich man's table. Even the dogs came and licked his sores. 22 The time came when the beggar died and the angels carried him to Abraham's side. The rich man also died and was buried. 23 In hell, where he was in torment, he looked up and saw Abraham far away, with Lazarus by his side. 24 So he called to him, 'Father Abraham, have pity on me and send Lazarus to dip the tip of his finger in water and cool my tongue, because I am in agony in this fire.' 25 But Abraham replied, 'Son, remember that in your lifetime you

received your good things, while Lazarus received bad things, but now he is comforted here and you are in agony. 26 And besides all this, between us and you a great chasm has been fixed, so that those who want to go from here to you cannot, nor can anyone cross over from there to us.' 27 He answered, 'Then I beg you, father, send Lazarus to my father's house, 28 for I have five brothers. Let him warn them, so that they will not also come to this place of torment.' 29 Abraham replied, 'They have Moses and the Prophets; let them listen to them.' 30 'No, father Abraham,' he said, 'but if someone from the dead goes to them, they will repent.' 31He said, to him, 'If they do not listen to Moses and the Prophets, they will not be convinced even if someone rises from the dead.'

It is important to keep reminding myself that when I read the Gospels I must always be aware that Matthew copied almost all of Mark's Gospel and then added his own stories, gloss and spin [spin is not just a recent development by George W. Bush, Dick Cheney, Alistair Campbell and Tony Blair!]. Similarly Luke copied Matthew's Gospel almost in its entirety, and added his own stories, gloss and spin. All the Gospel writers used this 'copy and add technique' to meet the specific needs of the community and people to whom they were writing.

Here with the story of Lazarus and the rich man, there are a number of things to notice. First, neither Mark nor Matthew has this story of Lazarus and the rich man, and nor for that matter does the Gospel of Thomas. So, why does Luke add this story? Luke clearly attributes this story to Jesus while he was talking with the Pharisees, and as the Pharisees seemed to be in love with money [at least that is what Luke accuses them of in v.14 of this chapter] it seems to make sense for Luke the outsider to use this story here. But did Jesus really tell this story or is this Luke's explanatory fiction used to make a point about the problems for the rich when confronted by the Kingdom of God?

Secondly, we need to note that Lazarus, this poor beggar who sits at the door of the rich man's house and waits for crumbs from the table, dies. When he does so, according to Luke, he is carried away to a place of honor sitting next to Abraham. Here is further evidence that Luke clearly had learned the Hebrew Scriptures and traditions, for some Jews believed that heaven was a place where there was a continual banquet given by Yahweh God and the most important person present was the father of the Nation, none other than Abraham himself. However, according to Luke, the seat of honor next to Abraham was not for the rich and famous; nor was it for the spiritual leaders such as the Pharisees and the Sadducees. The seat of honor was reserved for this most repellent of beggars who was so weak that he did not, because he could not, fight off the dogs that licked his sores.

Not only was that a slap in the face of all the Pharisees who thought that they were the righteous ones and people like Lazarus were beyond the care of Yahweh God, but Luke goes on in his story to attack the rich man. When the rich man dies, he did not go as the Pharisees were expecting, to Yahweh's heavenly banquet. Instead, the rich man was assigned to hell, and in the torment of hell we have the roles reversed. The rich man – who had allowed the beggar Lazarus to wait for scraps from his table – now that same rich man is pleading for Lazarus to give him a drink to take away some of the pain of hell's fires.

Whether or not there is any Paradise life beyond this one is debatable, but Luke can only write from within his experience, culture and religious traditions. Luke uses this story to make the point that unless we heed the warnings in this life and act as people of compassion, the roles will be reversed in death. Then the rich, who used their wealth, position and power for themselves in this life, will be poor in the next life; and in the life to come the poor and the exploited will be rich. Those who said all the right words and who thought of themselves as righteous will find out that, by the ways in which they lived their lives, they were in fact the unrighteous. This is Luke's constant warning.

Even though the rich man pleads on behalf of his brothers that they be warned about their life-styles so that they may avoid what is happening to him, Abraham says that not even by going back from the dead will the brothers listen to the warning. Abraham added, "If they do not listen to Moses and the Prophets, they will not be convinced even if someone rises from the dead."

But that is not all. There is another Lazarus in the Christian Testament. The general consensus amongst Bible scholars seems to be that the Lazarus of Luke is not the same Lazarus of John, but Bishop Jack Spong points out that the name Lazarus occurs only twice in the Bible, so could it be that both Luke in this reading and John, in chapter 11:1 – 44, are referring to the same Lazarus?

To help us in our thinking on this question from Spong, there are three points to be remembered concerning John's Gospel:

1] it was the last in our canon of Scripture to have been written;

2] John's Gospel can be broken down into seventy-seven passages, of which forty-four passages are unique to John's Gospel, and a further twenty-three appear in the other three synoptic Gospels;

3] most of the overlaps between John's Gospel and the other three occur in the passages concerned with Holy Week.

Within these overlaps we have the story of Lazarus who, in John's Gospel, was the brother of Martha and Mary and a good friend of Jesus. In John's account Lazarus does not go as the guest of honor to sit beside Abraham, but Jesus himself raises this Lazarus from the dead.

Significantly, immediately after John finishes this story the next passage in John chapter 11:45 - 57 concerns the chief priests and Pharisees plotting now as to how they can rid themselves of Jesus. It seems to me that John's Gospel took Luke's unique story of Lazarus and updated it to explain that even this 'miracle' of Jesus is not enough for many people to believe – as the saying goes, "There is none so blind as those who refuse to see."

In both the Gospel accounts concerning Lazarus, the importance is that if we follow the ways and teachings of Jesus we will never be the same again, and likewise, others will be changed because we are being changed.

As always, I am not concerned in the least as to whether or not John took Luke's account and updated it, nor whether or not this story of Jesus raising Lazarus from the dead really happened. The important question as far as I am concerned is a simple one: "What is the meaning behind the stories of Lazarus?"

In Luke's account of Lazarus, the meaning concerns the way in which we live today – knowing the words of the Creeds and praying certain prayers are not what following the ways of Jesus are about. To follow the ways of Jesus means to live a life-style that puts the needs of others before our own needs; to protect the poor and the outsider; to feed the hungry and provide shelter for the homeless; to welcome the stranger; to challenge the powers and authorities when others are exploited; to confront any barriers that needlessly separate one from another. Following the ways of Jesus is about actions of love, mercy, justice and peace, and not just about knowing or reciting certain words.

In John's account of Lazarus, the meaning concerns the transformation of our lives as we follow the ways and teachings of Jesus. In the story Lazarus was transformed from corpse into life again; and we too can be transformed within ourselves and in our dealings with others as we follow the ways and teachings of Jesus so that we can be raised daily from death to self [the corpse] to new life in Jesus. This is not an end of life experience but it is the way to live every day of our lives. It is the Eternal

Truth of the Easter stories: every small daily death to self by putting others first is followed by a resurrection to newness of life for us and for them.

Luke 18:1-8
The Parable of the Persistent Widow

> 1 Then Jesus told his disciples a parable to show them that they should always pray and not give up. 2 He said: "In a certain town there was a judge who neither feared God nor cared about men. 3 And there was a widow in that town who kept coming to him with the plea, 'Grant me justice against my adversary.' 4 For some time he refused. But finally he said, to himself, 'Even though I don't fear God or care about men, 5 yet because this widow keeps bothering me, I will see that she gets justice, so that she won't eventually wear me out with her coming!' 6 And the Lord said, 'Listen to what the unjust judge says. 7 And will not God bring about justice for his chosen ones, who cry out to him day and night? Will he keep putting them off? 8 I tell you, he will see that they get justice, and quickly. However, when the Son of Man comes, will he find faith on the earth?'

Luke 18:1-8 is another of those passages unique to Luke's Gospel and therefore I have to ask at least three questions: the first, 'If the other Gospel writers, including Thomas, did not write about this incident, did it really happen?' And second, 'Even if this story is only in the imagination of Luke, what was happening in Luke's community at the time of writing that made Luke think it was necessary to include this story?' And third, 'What may Luke's parable be saying to us today?'

I have great respect for the scholars who are members of what is known as the Jesus Seminar. However, I am a little uneasy with some of what they have to say concerning what is authentic and what is not authentic in the Gospels. Having said that, I do accept their scholarship that emphasizes some, but by no means all the parables and short words or statements of wisdom attributed to Jesus as being the nearest that we can get to what Jesus actually said. I am very happy to accept the Jesus Seminar scholars tendency to reject any parable or wisdom statement attributed to Jesus that speaks of judgment in general and of the end times and the Last Judgment in particular. These scholars conclude that such parables and one liner aphorisms are out of character with the rest of the life and teachings of Jesus. As such, they were later additions as the followers of the Way of Jesus were increasingly persecuted by both the Jews who rejected Jesus and by the Roman occupiers.

In my opinion it is important for us to go beyond the simplistic and yet long-taught idea that a parable is 'an earthly story with a heavenly meaning.' Two scholars, Dodd and Jeremias, are clear that each individual parable has a single point that it is making, and we should not interpret any parable as allegory – as a way in which we look at the characters and incidents to try to find deeper moral or Christian teaching. According to John Dominic Crossan, one of those Jesus Seminar scholars who has greatly influenced my theology, the parables were just simple stories designed to make people think beyond the wisdom of their times.

Then there is the work of the founder of the Jesus Seminar, Robert Funk. He took the line that the parables are metaphors of a different vision or alternative wisdom of Jesus, aimed at living differently in the here-and-now and not too concerned with what might be at the end of time. So what might this parable be about, included as it was in the Common Lectionary on the Sunday that ushered in 2007's One World Week?

In the parable there is the judge who fears no one, not even God, but he eventually gives in to the persistence of the widow. Is this a story about a judge and a widow, or is it about something else? Now if Luke was making some association between God and persistent prayer, then what a warped understanding Luke had of God! Such a God is time after time unmoved by the widow's plight – what kind of God is that? Such a God only gives in to stop the widow badgering him – this God seems very fickle to me, wanting the easy way out. Such a God as this will give into your prayer requests – if you pray long and hard enough. Now that is not the God that I know or would wish to follow! As far as I am concerned, this is not a parable about God – nor is it a parable about persistent prayer. And yet, how many sermons have we heard down the years that interpret this parable as being about persistent prayer?

Marcus Borg, in his book, *Jesus: A New Vision*, gives another insight into what this parable may be about. Borg says, "Jesus' perception of the broad way is also disclosed by the cast of characters in his parables. They realistically portray how human beings commonly act. Indeed, it is upon the skilful portrayal of typical human behavior that the power of the parable depends – the hearers recognize themselves."

If this is true then Luke may have created this parable and attributed it to Jesus, to help people of his community identify with the characters in the story. Perhaps in Luke's community there have been some dealings with an unjust judge and Luke is setting the record straight as to how and why the judge changed his mind? Perhaps there are some members who persistently badger others until they get their own way? Such an approach I call the 'rottweiler instinct' – once the teeth are in they just don't let go – and these people do exist, even in some churches!

Perhaps Luke was actually warning those people who persisted in prayer to the point of boredom that God actually wanted to give so much more than they were asking. In Luke's mind, in this situation God simply gives in and says, 'OK – if this is all you want, you've got it, now be off with you. But I wanted to give you so much more if only you would have been quiet for a moment.'

Or perhaps Luke is criticizing some of his community members for what Marcus Borg points out in that same book, "As snapshots of typical human behavior, the parables disclose much about Jesus' diagnosis of the human condition: we often are preoccupied with our concerns, anxious about our well-being, limited in our vision, grasping in our attempts to make ourselves secure." If Borg is right, then this parable is not about God, nor is it about persistent prayer, but it is about the weakness and frailty of the human condition, too selfishly concerned about ourselves to the extent that we forget about the needs of those around about us.

And in that, it maybe speaking directly to us today. If we are persistent and anxious pray-ers, concerned with our own needs, perhaps we are demonstrating less a depth or quality of faith, and more an unhealthy selfish concern about our trivial needs when the world – this One World – seems to be falling apart around us?

Over recent years in Britain there has been much heart searching about institutional and systemic racism in the police forces, especially in the wake of the murder of Stephen Lawrence on 22 April 1993 in Eltham, southeast London. Stephen was, at the time of his murder, an 18-year-old high school student. The police handling the case were subsequently accused of racism. Had Stephen been white rather than black then, the accusations went, the police would have dealt with the murder far more efficiently and treated the family of Stephen with greater respect and care. It was not until 31 July 1997 that Rt. Hon. Jack Straw announced the Macpherson inquiry into Stephen's death, "in order particularly to identify the lessons to be learned for the investigation and prosecution of racially motivated crimes." Sir William Macpherson presented his report in February 1999. But what has this to do with the parable of the persistent widow?

Perhaps we should be asking, as John Dominic Crossan

suggests, what would the hearers of the original telling of the parable been thinking? They probably would have known of an unjust judge. They probably were aware of a widow who was persistent in her demand for justice. The question that they may have been asking – and if they did not ask it then we should be asking it – "How could a system be allowed to develop in which judges are unjust and where widows, the poor, and the oppressed have to live in such intolerable conditions?" Perhaps this parable is not about a rottweiler of a widow but it is really about institutional and systemic injustice?

What was so different between the institutional and systemic injustice of Roman occupation then and the oppressive injustices today in places such as Zimbabwe, Israel/Palestine and Myanmar? When Luke was writing his Gospel it was difficult for the people to fight the institutional and systemic injustice of the time. It is also just as difficult for the pro-democracy demonstrators and Buddhist monks on the receiving end of the brutal military crackdown by the Myanmar junta in recent years. It has been just as difficult for the supporters of the pro-democracy movement in Zimbabwe who find themselves on the receiving end of Mugabe's tactics of brutality. It continues to be as difficult for Palestinians today who are still suffering the impact of the 1948 Nakba when Israeli forces committed ethnic cleansing of the Arab areas.

Dr Martin Luther King, writing from a prison cell in Birmingham, Alabama on 16th April 1963 said, "Injustice anywhere is a threat to justice everywhere." Perhaps the parable of the unjust judge and the persistent widow is a challenge to us to look again at what is going on in these situations and to take action on behalf of the people who are denied the fullness of life that Jesus offered to all? Perhaps this parable is a call to action and a challenge to injustice and corruption in which the poor and exploited need not be defeated forever?

Luke tells this parable some fifteen years or so after the disastrous rebellion of the Jews against the Romans. Therefore, through personal experience, Luke knew that brute force and military action was not the way to defeat the oppressors. Perhaps, therefore, the parable highlights that the way to challenge the corrupt and exploitative authorities is the way of non-violent persistent dialogue? For the powerless widow to challenge the unjust judge through persistent dialogue may just be the power that will work, because in her challenge the widow maintained her dignity and refused to accept the injustice of the judge no matter what the personal cost might have been.

Perhaps the message of this parable is the message that recent Governments in Britain have learned – the way to defeat the IRA was not by internment and military action but by dialogue? Perhaps the lesson from this parable is that the way to eventually bring peace and justice for all in Zimbabwe or the way to defeat the junta in Myanmar is by dialogue *and* not just by internationally imposed sanctions? It seems to me that too much foreign policy of the most powerful nations in the world today is based upon 'might is right – bomb them and sanction them into submission.' It applies just as much to the governments in Britain, the USA, Russia and Israel. It is a way that is doomed to failure. Perhaps the message of Luke to his original listeners was 'the dignity of persistent dialogue is always better than violence?'

That, surely, is the message for us who follow the ways of Jesus in these violent and oppressive times; and as we started 2007's One World Week, I challenged the members of the Church as to what we are doing about institutional and systemic injustice and oppression. I left the last comment to Sir Winston Churchill when speaking in the White House on 26th June 1954, "To jaw-jaw is better than to war-war." Has anything really changed over the centuries? I wonder, when will we learn that Perfect Love drives out all fear and prejudice - and the need to resort to violence?

Luke 18:9-14
The Parable of the Pharisee and the Tax Collector

9 To some who were confident of their own righteousness and looked down on everybody else, Jesus told this parable: 10 "Two men went up to the temple to pray, one a Pharisee and the other a tax collector. 11 The Pharisee stood up and prayed about himself: 'God, I thank you that I am not like other men—robbers, evildoers, adulterers—or even like this tax collector. 12 I fast twice a week and give a tenth of all I get.'

13 But the tax collector stood at a distance. He would not even look up to heaven, but beat his breast and said, 'God, have mercy on me, a sinner.'

14 I tell you that this man, rather than the other, went home justified before God. For everyone who exalts himself will be humbled, and he who humbles himself will be exalted."

Here in chapter 18, Luke introduces us to three parables attributed to Jesus, traditionally interpreted as concerning true discipleship that trusts in God the Father before whom there is the need for personal humility. First there is this parable of the Pharisee and the tax collector in which the pride of the Pharisee in doing all that he sees is required by the Law is contrasted with the humility of the tax collector, the one who is considered by the Pharisee to be rejected by God. The holiness code of the Pharisees encouraged them to believe that God blessed the righteous. And proof of such blessing was in an individual's prosperity, power, importance and influence, with the poor and outcast living proof that God did not bless them.

Then there follows the parable of the blessing of the little children in which the disciples try to turn the children back from approaching Jesus. Even now, after being with Jesus for some while, the disciples have yet to grasp that Jesus is concerned with openness and the equality of all in the Kingdom of God, including children and women, both the chattels of men.

And the third parable in this section on discipleship is the story of the rich man who keeps all the Law and yet still fails to follow Jesus because the social, political and economic benefits of his riches make it impossible for him to give up all and to take upon himself earthly poverty in exchange for heavenly blessing.

The traditional interpretation of all three of these discipleship parables is that those who wish to follow the Ways of Jesus should develop a humble faith in which they cast everything that they are and own into the care of God the Father.

But as we delve deeper into these three parables it should be noted that two of these, the blessing of the little children and the rich and important man, are found in the Gospel of Mark chapter 10 and its later copy in Matthew's Gospel chapter 19. But the parable of the Pharisee and the tax collector is unique to Luke, just as the preceding parable of the persistent widow and the unjust judge. So again, I have to ask if this is simply another of Luke's creations attributed to Jesus to meet a need or situation within the Lukan community?

Like the parable of the persistent widow and the unjust judge, the parable of the Pharisee and tax collector traditionally has been interpreted as being about the nature of prayer. However, just as Luke's unjust judge represented an abuse of the power structures of his day, so Luke developed this understanding by adding another slant to this parable, that of the pride of the self-righteous Pharisee. Traditionally, this has been interpreted in at least two ways. Firstly, as a challenge to the Followers of the Way of Jesus not to put our trust in our own abilities but rather to put our trust and faith in God.

Secondly, the challenge to us is to humble ourselves and to accept that in the Kingdom of God no one is to lord it over others, and no one is to look down upon any one else. I have no argument with such a conclusion, but my complaint is that the teachings of the Church down the centuries has unnecessarily spiritualized what was Luke's social commentary. Let us think again about the similarities between this parable and its preceding unjust judge and persistent widow story. Both parables are less about the nature of prayer and more to do with the frailty of human nature. This seems especially so to me when I note that in the thirty-three words of his prayer, the powerful, influential and self-righteous Pharisee asked nothing and needed nothing of God. His prayer was all about how good he was whereas the tax collector could find no more than seven words to express his sense of failure and sin before God.

Verse 13 says, "But the tax collector stood at a distance. He would not even look up to heaven, but beat his breast and said, 'God, have mercy on me, a sinner.'" Whereas the Pharisee wanted nothing from God, the tax collector wanted God's forgiveness. Luke really had it in for the Pharisee but more for what the caricatured Pharisee represented, the pride and divisive nature of social class. By the time Luke created this story and attributed it to Jesus, the Temple had been destroyed along with the whole Temple cult. Therefore, I think that Luke was probably writing these parables to highlight and to address Lukan community personalities and their problems with social status amongst the membership, carried over from the earlier pre-70 C.E. times.

Luke has this incident taking place at what had been the focal point of the religious consciousness of his Jewish listeners and readers, in the Jerusalem Temple. Luke the outsider had doubtless experienced the problems of arrogance and self-right-eousness that seemed to him to be the rotten core of Pharisaic Judaism. And although Luke does not set this story within his local community synagogue, perhaps by implication he is tackling similar problems at the centre of his own Christian community with its Jewish and Gentile followers of the Way of Jesus? This interpretation of the parable becomes more likely when coming to it with the approach of Marcus Borg who, you will remember, says that the importance and power of the parables is in individual listeners and readers recognizing themselves in the characters portrayed.

Although on the surface, Luke draws an obvious distinction between the prayers of the Pharisee and those of the tax collector, I think that this parable is more about social pride, social division and personal human nature than it is about the nature of prayer. I come to this conclusion because we see the Pharisee who thanked God that he was not like the lower and despised classes such as 'robbers, evildoers and adulterers - or even like this tax collector,' and the prayer of what one may call 'humble confession' of the lowly tax collector who knows his despised place within society. This tax collector has no sense of self-worth because others, and especially those who considered themselves to be righteous, rejected him and made him and those like him feel like dirt – unworthy and beyond the love and grace of God.

Can you imagine the gasps from Luke's listeners when they realized the turning upside down of social and religious conventions? As often happens in Luke's parables there are the 'goodies' and there are the contrasting 'baddies'. The predictable self-righteous understandings of the religious, along with their control over the social organization of the time, would have made a powerful socio-religious mix in which the Pharisee was seen as the one who was right in the sight of God, and the tax collector as the one who did not have God's favor.

In this parable Luke turns conventional wisdom and the social structures upside-down. The tax collector, a member of the reviled social underclass, is made the 'goodie' of the story and the holier-than-thou Pharisee becomes the 'baddie'.

It is like that famous BBC television 'That Was The Week That Was' sketch from the 1960s in which John Cleese, the tall one representing the upper classes, looked down upon Ronnie Barker the middle-sized and middle class one, who then looked down again upon the shortest one, Ronnie Corbett, dressed in his working class overalls. Cleese said somewhat contemptuously, 'I look down on both of these.' And then Ronnie Barker looked up at Cleese and said 'I look up to him' and then down to Corbett and said, 'but I look down on him.' And then at the end of the sketch, Ronnie Corbett looked up at both and said forlornly, 'I know my place.'

For any one to be made to believe that they are of no social significance, having nothing of importance to give to everyday life in either their family or community situations is not only a direct attack upon all that Jesus of Nazareth believed in and lived for, but it really is a crime against humanity. The narratives of the Gospel writers were commentaries upon both the oral stories about the Jesus of history and their own experiences of the impact of the on-going 'Jesus Presence' as the one who gave all and sundry a sense of self-worth and a promise that no matter who they were, life in an abundant fullness could be theirs regardless of the socio-economic and religious norms of the time. After all, this is what John's Gospel chapter 10 and verse 10 attributes to Jesus: "I have come that they may have life, and have it to the full." That must have been the experience of the Community that followed the teachings of John, a life of spiritual abundance amidst the oppression of Roman occupation and rejection from the synagogues.

Although Luke's story is set in the time of Jesus and the Jerusalem Temple, not even the Pharisee in the story is beyond the unconditional love that is God. After all, the Pharisee was sincere in following the rules of twice-weekly fasting, and tithing 10% of his earnings to the work of the Temple. And perhaps Luke was saying to his community, "Even though this Pharisee got it so wrong, he and other Pharisees were generous and without them the work of the Temple would have suffered. I am not condemning the Pharisee's generosity but it is his reason for fasting and giving that was so badly wrong."

In Luke's understanding, the Pharisee's hand was generous but his concerns were far from the unconditional and unassuming nature that would have enabled him to accept all people as equals in God's Kingdom. The generosity of the Pharisee could not be condemned but Luke did criticize his belief that by separating himself from the tax collector he was made righteous in the sight of God. The Pharisee constantly made the tax collector conscious of his countless failings and therefore of his desperate need to confess and to commit to following the Pharisaic ways. Sadly, these Pharisaic ways were erroneously equated with God's ways. Luke could not have made the contrast any greater!

Perhaps in Luke's community there were those who acted like the Pharisee in the parable, saying one thing and following all the rules, but whose lives were a lie to the truth that they were proclaiming? If this was so, think of the gasps as the listeners realized to whom Luke was referring. Perhaps Luke was shaming rather than naming members of his community who thought that discipleship was only about giving money rather than living a life that imitated Jesus and thus truly honored God? Perhaps Luke had to contend with financially or socially richer members of his community, or even those with a Pharisaic upbringing, who thought too much of themselves, and as more important than the poor and socially rejected?

To ensure that this message hit home, Luke attributed the dire warning to Jesus at the end of the parable, verse 14, "I tell you that the tax collector, rather than the Pharisee, went home justified before God." And here is the critically important sentence in the whole of this parable, "For everyone who exalts himself will be humbled, and he who humbles himself will be exalted."

This parable is not about the nature of prayer but it is about humility and the unconditional acceptance of the value of one another. As I see it, any Church today has to be open and welcoming of all who come. That means welcoming properly without any sense of superiority, those with criminal records;

adulterers; tax collectors; those who are HIV/AIDS sufferers; unmarried mothers and their children; black and white; the migrant and the refugee; the homeless and the helpless; the hungry; the gays and the straight – all should be equally welcome because all are temples of the Spirit of God. To welcome those who are different to us is the Gospel imperative and we should not expect 'them' to become like 'us' before we truly accept them amongst us.

The abundant life of which Jesus speaks comes to us in those whom we welcome; it is not something that is given to us just because we pray some prayer or other. It is in our unconditional welcome and acceptance of both ourselves and of others that we find abundant life for all.

There is no place in the Church for negative superiority that leads to division and rejection. The qualities that are needed are to honor and practice of what the British Chief Rabbi Jonathan Sacks calls 'the dignity of difference.' To do so will make all our lives not only better but also abundantly better. And as such, this parable is both up-to-date and relevant, speaking to us as individuals, as a church and as a nation.

Luke 19: 1 – 10
Zacchaeus the Tax Collector

1 Jesus entered Jericho and was passing through. 2 A man was there by the name of Zacchaeus; he was a chief tax collector and was wealthy. 3 He wanted to see who Jesus was, but being a short man he could not, because of the crowd. 4 So he ran ahead and climbed a sycamore-fig tree to see him, since Jesus was coming that way. 5 When Jesus reached the spot, he looked up and said to him, "Zacchaeus, come down immediately. I must stay at your house today." 6 So he came down at once and welcomed him gladly. 7 All the people saw this and began to mutter, "He has gone to be the guest of a 'sinner.' " 8

But Zacchaeus stood up and said to the Lord, "Look, Lord! Here and now I give half of my possessions to the poor, and if I have cheated anybody out of anything, I will pay back four times the amount." 9 Jesus said to him, "Today salvation has come to this house, because this man, too, is a son of Abraham. 10 For the Son of Man came to seek and to save what was lost."

I am occasionally challenged as to why I find it necessary to deconstruct – to take apart the traditional and comforting understandings and interpretations of Bible stories and the Creeds of the Christian Church. I do so out of love and concern for the present and for the future of the Church. It is those very traditional and comforting understandings and interpretations that the majority of people in Britain, let alone in Europe and North America and Australasia, have rejected as irrelevant to life in this post-modern world. Unless we bring contemporary scholarship to bear upon the traditional and comforting understandings and interpretations of the Church then there is no long-term future for the Church.

But even more than for the Church, I am concerned for the future of all that Jesus represents in the fullness of Humanity and the fullness of Divinity. Without the presence of the Spirit of Jesus the future of society as we know it, let alone the long-term future of humankind, is put at risk. Like it or not, we are either at the forefront of a new reformation of the Christian Church, or we are in the midst of its death throes.

I believe this is the seriousness of the situation that the Church and we are in. It is no good that anyone says, "As long as the death of the Church happens after I have passed on, then I am quite happy." We owe it to our children, grandchildren and for the generations to come to ensure that there is a Church that continues to impact with the message of God in Jesus. However, I sometimes wonder if it is not already too late even for progressive Christianity to arrest the decline. Perhaps the Church is already in a state of perilous decay from which there is no return? If this is the case then we must find another way to encourage and support spirituality devoid of institutional religion.

Therefore I make no apology for what I am saying here about Zacchaeus, even though it may cause upset for a number of people because I may be shattering an important Bible story that they have held onto as somehow comforting and reassuring since they were children.

It is very possible that there was a small man who climbed a tree to see Jesus over the heads of the crowd. It is definitely possible that Jesus and his disciples went home with a small man and enjoyed having afternoon tea with him. And it is perfectly acceptable if there are those who want to hang onto this wonderful story of unconditional acceptance, unreserved hospitality and a repentance that truly cost, because no matter how we interpret this story, that remains the underlying Eternal Truth – that the Perfect Love that is God demonstrates in Jesus that we are accepted as we are and calls us to offer similar unconditional generosity to the extent that there will be a personal cost to us.

Love them or loathe them, tax collectors were very important in the life and experience of Luke. In his previous chapter Luke wrote about the Pharisee and the nameless tax collector, and now he introduced the listeners and readers to another tax collector. This time it is no ordinary tax collector but a chief tax collector. Similarly, this time it is not an anonymous tax collector but one named Zacchaeus.

Notice that Luke set this story in Jericho, now on the Palestinian West Bank. However, Luke was probably writing in his native Antioch in present day Turkey. In a straight line these two cities are some 300 miles apart, but the journey would have been far longer then, traveling from Jericho on foot, probably north along the Jordan Valley, through Galilee and then at

Caesarea Philippi, turning west to Tyre on the Mediterranean Sea, and from there the second half of the journey probably would have been made by ship.

At the time of Jesus, Antioch was the capital of Roman occupied Syria and the third largest city of the entire Roman Empire. Consequently there was wealth attracted to the city and therefore a number of tax collectors would have been resident. But also attracted to Antioch was a significant number of Followers of the Way of Jesus who fled from Jerusalem as a result of the stoning to death of Stephen, a martyrdom supported by Saul of Tarsus who went on to become the Apostle Paul.

As a result of their witness and open communal life style, these exiled Jerusalem believers became the catalysts in the conversion of many gentile Greeks and the Messianic fulfillment for many Jews. This made the Church community in Antioch second only to that in Jerusalem.

So why did Luke, over half a century later, have such an interest in tax collectors? Once again, why are these stories of tax collectors unique to Luke's Gospel? As they were unknown to Thomas, Paul, Peter, Mark, Matthew, and whatever might have been the Q source, I have to ask again, 'Was Zacchaeus a real person?' And the answer is that I doubt that there was a man called Zacchaeus who met and had tea with Jesus. But perhaps Luke had a generous tax collector within his community whom he disguised by naming him Zacchaeus?

So now I come to pin prick the balloon of childhood memories of singing the Sunday School song "Zacchaeus was a very little man and a very little man was he!" If Zacchaeus had been a real person who had this extraordinary afternoon tea with Jesus, why was Luke alone in spelling out this repentance and generosity of spirit? Surely, any wealthy repentant sinner who gave half his riches to the poor and, from the other half, he repaid four times as much of whatever he cheated from people, would have entered not only the Lukan community's folklore over the intervening fifty years but would have been wide spread knowledge throughout the Christian communities in Jericho, Jerusalem, Antioch and elsewhere? Surely if this was a genuine historic event, the Jesus/Zacchaeus incident would have made it into the Gospels of Mark and Matthew and the early writings of Peter and Paul?

As this probably was a fictitious story of Zacchaeus, but possibly based upon someone within Luke's community, why did Luke choose to set it in Jericho, an oasis 300 miles away in the middle of the desert? Perhaps Luke selected Jericho because this was known throughout these Roman-occupied provinces as a parallel to Antioch as both a wealthy trading centre and a city of strategic importance to the Roman occupiers? But it was also a place of anonymity. Perhaps Jericho was selected not to embarrass or to give away a secret donation by a repentant tax collector who had joined Luke's community?

But there were probably other reasons also for this choice of venue. Before the destruction of the Temple in 70 C.E., Jericho had also been an important resting point for pilgrims from Galilee on their 80-mile trek to Jerusalem. Indeed, Jesus visited Jericho on his final walk to Jerusalem and it may or may not be significant, but considering the part played by palm trees at the start of that final week in the life of Jesus, Jericho, just 15 miles from Jerusalem, was known as the 'City of Palms.' So could it have been that the palm-waving events of Palm Sunday had actually taken place days before whilst Jesus traveled through Jericho en route for that fateful week in Jerusalem? If so, the Gospel writers retold history remembered and placed it into the Jerusalem part of the Easter narrative for dramatic effect.

But think again as to why Luke referred to this fictitious wealthy chief tax collector by the name 'Zacchaeus'. At that time tax collectors were Jewish collaborators with the Roman oppressors. They were seen as those who cheated their own people by charging the Roman tax and adding something extra for themselves. This made Zacchaeus extremely wealthy and thus even more despised by the local Jewish population.

Again, according to Luke, Zacchaeus was the chief of the tax collectors. Some people read this as 'chief by eminence' but I prefer a different approach in which Zacchaeus was chief by the level of sleaze amongst the tax collectors in Jericho. But here is the major clue as to why I think that Zacchaeus was less a real person and more a handiwork of Luke's imagination when he named this chief tax collector. The Greek name 'Zacchaeus' is the masculine form from the Hebrew name 'Zakhhay' meaning 'pure'.

How strange that anyone who is considered to be the lowest of the low and the most corrupt of the corrupted should be named 'pure'? What an amazing coincidence and how ironic if this was a genuine name of a real person – the despised lowest of the low, the social outcast, named 'pure'!

Please read this paragraph carefully as this is the key, not only to these tax collector stories but to the whole of Luke's writings: the Jewish members of Luke's community would have known that Luke was playing with words. Sadly, the problem was with the Gentile members of that community who did not understand the creative way in which the Jews told their stories and interpreted their Scriptures.

Whereas the Jewish listeners and readers would have known that these tax collector stories were Lukan parables, the Gentiles heard and read them as history remembered. And that has been the problem of Scriptural interpretation ever since. The Greek Gentile minds that came to dominate the Christian churches by the end of the first century have literalized what were analogy, metaphor, Midrash and parable. While we continue to do that, we miss the real concerns and intentions of Luke when he wrote his two-part Good News of Jesus: first in his Gospel and then of the ongoing impact of Jesus in the history of the early Church communities in the Acts of the Apostles.

Far from history remembered, I think that, with his unique 'outsider' parables, Luke is making a point to his ninth decade community, that no matter how much the community rejected a person, in the values of the Kingdom even the lowest of the low is unconditionally accepted and considered to be 'pure.'

I wonder if Luke was rehearsing what he was to write in the Acts of the Apostles, in which he highlighted the example of the Jerusalem community of Christians where, soon after the first Easter and Christian Pentecost, the wealthy gave all they had to the community so that all was held in common and for the common good? Was Luke reminding his community of what the early exiles from Jerusalem had brought with them, 'all for one and one for all'?

Or perhaps there is another explanation for this parable? Perhaps Luke was publicly using a fictitious name, 'Zacchaeus', [the 'pure one'] to back into a corner a wealthy tax collector who had recently joined the community but had, as yet, not opened his purse strings? Perhaps we shall never know, but from my studies I think that Luke created both the character 'Zacchaeus' and this Jesus/Zacchaeus incident not just to make a spiritual point that Perfect Love covers all people, but, as I have previously stated in the analysis of the fictitious parable of the Pharisee and the tax collector, it was also a social commentary upon Luke's community of believers in Antioch some fifty years after the first Easter.

Therefore, if this story was created within Luke's imagination, does it have any relevance to us today? And the answer to that is an emphatic 'Yes'! Perhaps the Eternal Spirit is continuing to say to us, through the Luke examples of the tax collectors who were social outsiders, "No one is beyond Sacred Grace and therefore all are welcome into and must not be excluded from our present day Christian communities!"

We will never get into our churches those whom society might consider to be the lowest of the low unless we welcome them in such a way that we give them a sense of self-worth both within the Sacred and within our communities of believers.

Jesus, our exemplar, accepted the lowest of the low and we, too, should be open to all regardless of who or what they are or what they have been. Luke's stories of the tax collectors carry the same message of unconditional acceptance and openness towards all people all of the time no matter what the personal cost. No matter how we interpret this story, the underlying truth is that Sacred Grace unconditionally accepts us as we are and calls us to take the risk and, in and through the Church, to offer unconditional hospitality to all.

However, in these days it is a risk for any one, especially for the elderly, to welcome unconditionally just any body into our homes. In my situation, as a Methodist Minister, I have to abide by Standing Orders of the British Methodist Church. Therefore, should any one come to the local Church who has a Court Supervision Order having been found guilty of child abuse, the welcome must be within the control conditions placed upon them to protect them as well as our children and other vulnerable adults. But, within those legal constraints we should welcome unconditionally so that the Church community is an open place in which unconditional love and unconditional acceptance is available and offered to all. It is the Way of Jesus and it must be the way of the Church.

Chapter Four

Jesus In Jerusalem And Beyond

Luke 21:5-19
Signs of the End of the Age

5 Some of his disciples were remarking about how the temple was adorned with beautiful stones and with gifts dedicated to God. But Jesus said, 6 "As for what you see here, the time will come when not one stone will be left on another; every one of them will be thrown down." 7 "Teacher," they asked, "when will these things happen? And what will be the sign that they are about to take place?" 8 He replied: "Watch out that you are not deceived. For many will come in my name, claiming, 'I am he,' and, 'The time is near.' Do not follow them. 9 When you hear of wars and revolutions, do not be frightened. These things must happen first, but the end will not come right away." 10 Then he said to them: "Nation will rise against nation, and kingdom against kingdom. 11 There will be great earthquakes, famines and pestilences in various places, and fearful events and great signs from heaven. 12 But before all this, they will lay hands on you and persecute you. They will deliver you to synagogues and prisons, and you will be brought before kings and governors, and all on account of my name. 13 This will result in your being witnesses to them. 14 But make up your mind not to worry beforehand how you will defend yourselves. 15 For I will give you words and wisdom that none of your adversaries will be able to resist or contradict. 16 You will be betrayed even by parents, brothers, relatives and friends, and they will put some of you to death. 17 All men will hate you because of me. 18 But not a hair of

your head will perish. 19 By standing firm you will gain life."

We are now into the final week of the life of Jesus. From the various, and sometimes contradictory, Gospel accounts, the visits to the Temple became daily events in which Jesus taught those who were prepared to listen until what we now call Maundy Thursday. But in the process, Jesus had upset the status quo in Jerusalem, and questions concerning his authority were being asked once again by the chief priests, teachers of the Law and finally by the Roman political and military leadership. The challenge to Jesus concerning paying of taxes to Caesar or to God has past. Once again Jesus is back in the Temple and Luke chapter 21 starts with the story of the widow's mite.This poor woman contributed everything from her poverty while the rich gave much more money but only of what they did not need. And Jesus turned the accepted wisdom of the day the right way up. He praised the poor woman and criticized the rich.

But there is more to Luke chapter 21 than meets the eye, and to get under the story we need some background information. Have you noticed how the same passages of Scripture are often section-by-section sub-titled differently across a range of Bible translations, reflecting different theological understandings as to what the passage of Scripture is really getting at? Luke 21:5-19 is one of those passages.

The New American Standard Bible, first published in 1960, starts not at v5 but at v1 with the story of the widow's gift [or the 'widow's mite'] and it continues the setting of the widow's story in the Jerusalem Temple so that the warnings attributed to Jesus about the destruction of the Temple flow naturally from the story of the widow's mite. It is at v10 when the emphasis and title change into 'Things to come'.

There is the 'love it or hate it' translation called 'The Message', first published in 1993, where the whole section from v5 to v19 is entitled 'Watch Out for Doomsday Deceivers'. In the

New Living Translation, first published in 1996, this same section is entitled 'Jesus foretells the future'.

The Contemporary English Version, first published in 1995, separates the sections into v5 to v7 entitled 'The Temple will be destroyed' and v8 to v19 'Warning about trouble'. And then there is the English Standard Version, first published in 2001, in which v5 to v9 is entitled 'Jesus foretells the destruction of the Temple' and then v10 to v19 switches to 'Jesus foretells wars and persecution.' There are other translations that approach this whole passage from v5 to v19 as one continuous story. For example, in the New International Version of the Bible, first published in 1973, this section is entitled 'Signs of the End of the Age'.

Those who claim that the only real Bible is the King James Version, first published in 1611, are saved from all this erudition as there are no section titles, just the numbering of chapters; and when taken at face value, even though the translators interpret and therefore sub-title sections differently, the common themes seem to be those of forewarning of the destruction of the Temple, disaster for the nation, and protection for those who follow and remain faithful to Jesus.

But there is still more to this passage than mere face value. Luke 21:5-19 is paralleled in Mark chapter 13:1-13 and in Gospel of Matthew chapter 24:1-14, both written before Luke's Gospel. But none of these parallel verses appear in the earlier Gospel of Thomas and so I conclude, based upon my research of recent Biblical scholarship, Jesus may not have said any thing specifically about the destruction of the Temple. However, saying 72 of the earlier Gospel of Thomas mentions a house destroyed that no one can rebuild; but this is part of a saying directed at the brothers of Jesus in which Jesus asks that his brothers share with him the possessions of his, presumably, dead father. Perhaps, again with the benefit of Gospel hindsight, Matthew and Luke later adapted this saying and then attributed it to Jesus, applying it as history to the Temple's destruction at the hands of Roman occupiers? Or maybe both Matthew and Luke were using a similar source that had not been used by Thomas or Mark?

I willingly concede that the pragmatic Jesus probably said something more generally along the lines of what would happen as a result of the impending disaster and persecution arising from Roman occupation. Indeed, saying 16 of Thomas records Jesus warning that fathers and sons will fight against each other as recorded by Luke chapter 21:v1, "You will be betrayed even by parents, brothers, relatives and friends." Similarly, saying 18 of Thomas reassures the Followers of the Way of Jesus that they will not taste death, just as Luke's Gospel chapter 21:19 reassures his community members that they will gain life. Saying 69 of Thomas warns of persecution, but reassures the readers and hearers that such persecution will be a blessing for the Followers of the Way of Jesus.

This historical background is vital to our understanding of Luke chapter 21:5-19, because it helps us in our consideration of one of Luke's primary sources, Mark's Gospel. But it is also important in helping us to understand that, along with its Mark parallel, Luke chapter 21:5-19 is one of those passages that divide scholars as to the dating of the writing of Mark's Gospel.

One approach is that the Gospel attributed to Mark was written in the years 64 to 67 C.E. in Rome, shortly after the execution of Peter. This tradition goes back to Papias Bishop of Hierapolis writing early in the second century. If Papias was correct, then the Gospel of Mark was indeed foretelling what would happen should the Christians and Jews rise up against Rome. The signs were easy to see – the result of rebellion against Rome would be another disaster for the Jewish people. But there was nothing new in what Jesus was recorded as having said – deceivers, wars, famines, and so on. Such things were and always have been part of what it means to be not yet fully human.

This pre-70 C.E. tradition is supported by the fact that Mark's Gospel chapter 13 speaks of the end times but does not specifically mention the destruction of the Temple. So it can be deduced that although the writer of Mark's Gospel was able to accurately guess the disastrous outcome of any rebellion against Rome, he had no knowledge of the destruction of the Temple. That has to be a later Matthew and then a Luke addition to the Mark story, written with the benefit of hindsight and recent history.

The uncertainty over the dating of Mark's Gospel can be seen in the research of Jesus Seminarians such as Bishop Jack Spong and Marcus Borg. In his book *Jesus: A New Vision* [1987, 170], Borg suggests that Mark may have been written as early as 65. However, in *Meeting Jesus again for the First Time*, [1994, p.18] Borg writes, "The most widely accepted scholarly understanding is that Mark is the earliest Gospel, written around A.D. 70." However, I am unsure if this '70 thesis' places this before, during or immediately after the destruction of the Temple. The answer to that could be crucial with regard to the implications for the interpretation of Mark's Gospel as a whole.

The uncertainty continues with Bishop Jack Spong. In his book, *Rescuing the Bible from Fundamentalism* [1991, p. 82], he says, "Mark is usually dated no earlier than 65 C.E and no later than 75." But a year later, Spong placed the writing of Mark's Gospel "35 to 40 years after the Easter moment" [*Born of a Woman*, 1992, p.54]. If that first Easter was in 33 or 34 C.E., then Mark's Gospel was written between 68 and 74. Either way, such dating conveniently dodges the question as to whether or not Mark knew about the destruction of the Temple and the disastrous defeat of the Jewish rebellion that ended with the mass suicide of Jewish fighters at Masada on 16th April 73 C.E.

If the Gospel of Mark was written as late as 74 or 75, the writer was looking back with hindsight and was thus able to write into the mouth of Jesus 'the signs of the times' and the forewarnings of persecution some 40 years before the actual events took place.

However, whether or not Mark is pre or post 70 C.E., by the time that the Gospels of Matthew and Luke were written, the story of Jesus telling of the impending destruction of the Temple had been added. Additionally, the story of the Temple Curtain being torn from top down at the moment of the death of Jesus occurs in Mark 15:38, suggesting evidence that it might have been written post-70 C.E.

In correspondence with Jack Spong he told me that he favors a later date for the writing of Mark's Gospel, "I date Mark after 70. Not only do I think chapter 13 is putting the prediction of the fall of Jerusalem into Jesus' mouth, but I also think the story of the transfiguration, which Mark introduces, would be impossible prior to the destruction of the Temple. In that story, Jesus has replaced the Temple as the meeting place between God and human life and the light of God usually focused on the Temple is now focused on Jesus."

And who am I to disagree with his scholarship? But on this issue I prefer to think differently. I am with the tradition that places Mark's Gospel earlier rather than later. After all, if Mark's Gospel was written after the destruction of the Temple, why is there no specific mention of its destruction and the end of the Temple Cult?

Of any of these things we cannot be totally certain. We have few independent writers during the life of Jesus and the early years of the Christian movement. Often we have only tradition, folklore and Christian Testament records on which to base our conclusions. For example, a tradition that is pertinent to this study in Luke chapter 21 concerns the years in which Peter was in Rome. This tradition is traced back to Jerome, the late fourth and early fifth century monk and scholar. Jerome wrote that Peter, as the first Pope, laid the foundation stones to a great Church in Rome in the year 42 C.E.

Independent historic records show that Emperor Claudius then expelled all Jews from Rome in the years 49 and 50. It cannot be verified that Peter had or had not been in Rome at the time of this expulsion. However he was in Jerusalem and was party to the Council of Jerusalem in 50 C.E. It was this early Council that decided in favor of the Apostle Paul and the Gentile Followers of Jesus. No longer were Gentile 'Christian' converts subjected to the Mosaic Law that included circumcision: in other words, the practice ceased in which Gentile converts to Jesus were made to become Jews first!

As Christians we so often miss the importance of this Council of Jerusalem. Although the final split between Judaism and Christianity was still to come over the following three to four decades, this was the beginning of the end of the acceptance and accommodation of Christian Jews and Christian Gentiles worshipping together with Jews who rejected the Jesus message. Here again is another example that once the questions start [in this case "How can Jew and Gentile, Jew and Christian continue to worship together in the synagogue?"] the only ultimate question is "How long will it take?" Once the status quo is questioned, the outcome is inevitable and change will take place at some point in the future. This reasoning also applies today to the theology of progressive Christianity. It is only time before the progressives usurp the power and influence of the literalists and fundamentalists within the institutional Church.

Emperor Claudius died in 54, and perhaps it was then that Peter went either for the first time or returned to Rome, perhaps thinking that persecution was over? However, persecution of Christian Followers of the Way of Jesus the Jew came again when Emperor Nero accused the Christians of intentionally causing the Great Fire of Rome. According to the historian Tacitus, who was 9 years old at the time of the fire, the fire began on 18th July 64 C.E. Both Peter and Paul were executed in the persecution that followed that Great Fire.

If Jesus had really answered as Mark, Matthew and Luke record then I can also imagine some of those original listeners, especially the Pharisees and the Sadducees, treating Jesus as an impostor. "Oh yes Jesus, we know that there are wars and rumours of wars, look how we are under Roman occupation because we lost the war! And revolution? There are Zealots all around us who constantly attack the Romans and stir up trouble for us all. Tell us something that we don't know. And by the way, we know that nation will rise against nation, and kingdom against kingdom – that's why we are prisoners in our own country. And we know about great earthquakes, wasn't there one at Qumran sixty years ago? And famine? Don't give us that one – we live on famine rations all the time!"

And so on, and so on. But if we put these signs, plus the added comments about the impending destruction of the Temple, into the context of the writing of the Gospels of Matthew and Luke some fifty years after the first Easter , then things begin to take on a different significance. Now we see the Followers of the Way of Jesus looking back and realizing what had happened. Indeed many deceivers had come in the name of Jesus, claiming, 'I am he,' and, 'The time is near.' In the Book of Acts, not yet written but the content obviously known to Luke and doubtless already used by him as a warning to his community, Luke has the story of Paul and Barnabas encountering Elymas Bar-Jesus meaning 'Elymas son of Jesus' when they reached Cyprus [Acts chapter 13]. Elymas meant 'magician' or 'corrupter' – the 'corrupting son of Jesus'! Mark, Matthew and Luke all warn the believers in their communities not to follow any one who claims to be the new or the returned Jesus. Or could this Elymas be the son of Jesus and Mary Magdalene, but now corrupting the message and exploiting his family status? But that is a specu-lation that is a step too far for today!

But what about those 'signs of the times'? Followers of the Way of Jesus in the Matthew and Luke communities would have been fully aware of war and revolution. Many would have been the survivors or immediate descendants of the survivors of the

Judean uprising between 66 and 73. The encouragement to the Followers of the Way of Jesus was, "Even in these dark times of oppression and persecution, do not be frightened because God is with you."

And earthquakes and the like? Perhaps the news of the eruption of Vesuvius on August 23-24 in the year 69 C.E. had reached this part of the Roman Empire in which the Gospels of Matthew and Luke were written. They would almost certainly have within their oral folklore the story of the Qumran earthquake in 31 B.C.E. These events had happened and would happen again.

As for famine – there had been a great famine throughout the Roman Empire, including Judea from 42 to 44 C.E. and again from 49 to 52 C.E. This would have been in the Judean folklore. The church in Antioch is recorded in Acts chapter 11 as having sent famine relief to the Jerusalem Church in 43 C.E.

By the time that Mark, Matthew and Luke were writing their Gospels, persecution had been a major experience of the Followers of the Way of Jesus. Church leaders, including many of the original disciples of Jesus, had been martyred, beginning with Stephen by stoning, and shortly after of James, the son of Zebedee and the brother of John, by beheading. All these events contributed to the Diaspora that spread the good news of Jesus from its home in Jerusalem and Judea throughout the Middle East as Followers of the Way of Jesus fled the religious persecution in Jerusalem. Evidence as to the extent of the decimation of the early Church leadership can be found in the writings of Hippolytus, the 2nd century Christian writer who stated that James the son of Alphaeus was also stoned to death as the result of preaching in Jerusalem; Andrew was crucified in Greece; Bartholomew was crucified in Armenia; James the brother of John was killed by the sword in Judea; Philip was crucified in Hierapolis; Thomas was killed in India.

Then Eusebius, the early 4th century Bishop of Caesarea and

historian of the early churches, also claimed that Peter had been executed in Rome. Many Followers of the Way of Jesus had been brought before kings and governors. There was nothing new in this.

When both the Gospels of Matthew and Luke were being written, the Followers of the Way of Jesus, both Jew and Gentile, were being systematically ejected from the synagogues. The early churches all knew and many members would have experienced persecution. But, if there was no substance to the message of encouragement and support contained in verses 18 and 19 of this chapter, "But not a hair of your head will perish. By standing firm you will gain life," then why should the people have remained Followers of the Jesus Movement?

As I read about the Early Church communities I conclude that their success was not based upon a set of Creedal beliefs – the Creeds of the Church had not yet been written! The strength and power that fuelled the growth of the early churches against all the odds was the way in which they lived. It was not in what they said but it was in the way they loved and cared for one another; it was the way of sharing the little that they had so no one need go hungry. It was a commitment to equality and social justice.

We now know that God is no more above the sky than we are; that the world is not flat; that the Devil and Hell are not just below our feet. We only need to look at television news to know that Heaven and Hell are not simply about experiences beyond death but they are very real amongst us now. Two-thirds of the world will go to bed hungry tonight – that is Hell enough for them. If the people in the early churches did not also experience the life force of Jesus in their caring and sharing for one another, then why should they have become missionary-minded? Why should they have invited others to join in the life giving, life-enhancing experience of the Spirit of God found so completely in Jesus of Nazareth?

If the invited came and failed to find the Spirit that gives

Living Water to the spiritually thirsty, then the Churches would not have grown. If the persecuted, oppressed and hungry did not find the depth of love, support and encouragement lived and not just spoken about amongst the Followers of the Way of Jesus, then the Churches would have gone the way of all organizations that fail to deliver what they promise.

So what has all this to say to us today? It was the writer of Mark's Gospel, having taken oral tradition and the teachings and memories of Peter, who attributed to Jesus these words of comfort that all will be well. "Stand firm and receive life." These words were written in extremely dark times for the Followers of the Way of Jesus.

Later still, both Matthew and Luke took Mark chapter 13:1-13 to encourage and to reassure their community members who were Followers of the Way of Jesus that all would be well. This passage in Luke's Gospel chapter 21 was an encouragement to the Christians who were facing hunger, Roman persecution, oppression and exploitation, and Jewish expulsion from the synagogues. Yet they also experienced the on-going presence of Jesus in the love that was shared amongst the members of the Christian communities.

The Churches in Australasia, Britain, Europe and North America today are not oppressed or persecuted. Very few of its members are either hungry or thirsty. We have choices and we suffer from having too much rather than from having too little. And it seems to me that the more people possess the less they seem to need a 'personal' Sacred or the Church. A recent guest in our home was a Methodist Minister from a third world communist country. That was a humbling experience. The Church in that communist country is not as free as it is in Australasia, Britain, Europe and North America. The average wage is the equivalent of $20 per month and the diet extremely limited. Yet over these past ten years the number of Methodists in that country has grown from 7,000 to over 70,000. There are now over seventy ministers in training – more than in the Methodist Church in Britain! When asked why the church is growing in that country and why it seems to be dying in Britain, he responded with two statements, "British church services are boring. What you need to grow again is to have salsa in your worship."

I had to contradict him by replying, "The cultures of your country and of Britain are very different. To introduce salsa into our church services will empty the main stream churches even more quickly!"

However, where I agree with him is in his second statement, "We have gone back to the beginning. When we have nothing, we know that our only hope is in God."

The growing Church in that country is the result of living as those to whom the writers of Mark and Matthew and Luke addressed their Gospels. As music to the ears of present day Methodists, the Methodist Church in that country is modeling growth upon the Journals of John Wesley, in that the people are less organized within church buildings and greater concentration is placed upon the Wesley concept of Class Meetings [home-based communities of believers].

One of the major differences between the early primitive Church communities and our situation now is that they had too little and we have too much. Perhaps this is the message that we need to live – a message of sacrificial love for all our sisters and brothers in the One 'God' of All people, no matter where they are in this world: "Live simply that others may simply live." Perhaps that is the challenge to us all, not just to those in the Church, but to all communities where psychological, religious and social problems are the result of too much choice rather than of too little choice?

In a very real sense we are always living in the end times. The signs of the times – war, famine, deceit – are always similar and are always with us. But in spite of this, there is encouragement wherever we find our openness to the Spirit leading us to be more generous with ourselves and with others, within the bond of love in Jesus.

Even though the signs of the times may be far from what we would like – nuclear proliferation, religious extremism, terrorism, and global climate change – the promise is sure in that as we love one another as demonstrated 2000 years ago by Jesus we will experience life in all its emotional, psychological and spiritual abundance. It is the economy of God's Kingdom, that the more love we give away the more we will receive love. It is in the interests of the future of both the Christian Church and the whole of human kind, that we hear what the Spirit is saying to us.

And the significance of this for us? The traditional messages, teachings and Creeds have been continually designed and refined to bring about unity amongst those who wanted to belong, and to exclude all contrary opinion and experience. The major Creeds were written in times long gone and they tell us about the birth of Jesus and the death of Jesus but the really important part – the life of Jesus – is left out. To be a Follower of the Way of Jesus is not about Creedal statements – it's not even about books and sermons – but it is about the way in which we love one another in the Name of Jesus. The Christian faith and the Christian Church will not survive if the major concern is with who is in and who is out, based upon saying certain Creedal words and prayers. In the post-Enlightenment age in which we live, Creedal faith will not survive. And the institutional Church can survive only if its members return to non-creedal living in the Life and Power of Perfect Love demonstrated to us all by Jesus of Nazareth.

Luke 23:33 – 49
The execution of Jesus

When they came to the place called the Skull, there they crucified him, along with the criminals—one on his right, the other on his left. 34 Jesus said, "Father, forgive them, for they do not know what they are doing." And they divided up his clothes by casting lots. 35 The people stood watching, and the rulers even sneered at him. They said, "He saved others; let him save himself if he is the Christ of God, the Chosen One." 36 The soldiers also came up and mocked him. They offered him wine vinegar 37 and said, "If you are the king of the Jews, save yourself." 38 There was a written notice above him, which read: THIS IS THE KING OF THE JEWS. 39 One of the criminals who hung there hurled insults at him: "Aren't you the Christ? Save yourself and us!" 40 But the other criminal rebuked him. "Don't you fear God," he said, "since you are under the same sentence? 41 We are punished justly, for we are getting what our deeds deserve. But this man has done nothing wrong." 42 Then he said, "Jesus, remember me when you come into your kingdom." 43 Jesus answered him, "I tell you the truth, today you will be with me in paradise."

44 It was now about the sixth hour, and darkness came over the whole land until the ninth hour, 45 for the sun stopped shining. And the curtain of the temple was torn in two. 46 Jesus called out with a loud voice, "Father, into your hands I commit my spirit." When he had said this, he breathed his last.

47 The centurion, seeing what had happened, praised God and said, "Surely this was a righteous man." 48 When all the people who had gathered to witness this sight saw what took place, they beat their breasts and went away. 49 But all those who knew him, including the women who had followed him from Galilee, stood at a distance, watching these things.

I wonder why both the Gospel of Mark and that of Matthew have the story of the two criminals who are executed either side of Jesus, verbally attacking Jesus, but in Luke's Gospel one of the criminals being executed turns to Jesus and pleads, "Remember me when you come into your Kingdom."

If there was ever an example to prove that the Bible should not be read literally then this is it! How can the Bible be infallible and without error, God's spoken Word for Word, when there are contradictory accounts of the same story of the criminals executed alongside Jesus?

In the traditional teachings of the Church, where Jesus is seen both as the "Word made flesh," living amongst ordinary people, and as the "Only Son of God," then Jesus was born to die on Calvary's Cross. It is also the traditional teaching of the Church that New Life is now ours through the suffering, death, and resurrection of Jesus.

But there is another way of looking at the life and purpose of Jesus. I recently came across a sermon by Rex Hunt, a minister in the Uniting Church in Australia, who is influenced by much of the Jesus Seminar scholarship, delivered on Good Friday 2004, in which he said:

"The cross is about Jesus' integrity, not sacrificial atonement; God's love is not about supernatural payment or rescue, but divine sharing in human suffering; Jesus did not invite the cross but accepted it rather than abandon his vision or glimpse of what the world can really be like when you look at it with God's eyes."

I begin this section with the chronological order of the events on that far from 'Good' Friday. Mark begins this passage at about midday. He has the sky turning black and remaining that way until around 3 in the afternoon. Was Mark originally commenting on an eclipse of the sun? But that would have been moments of darkness, minutes maybe, but not three hours. Besides which, even though there are some suggestions that solar eclipses occurred in the region around Jerusalem in the years 27, 29, 30, 33 and 34 C.E., there seem to be no sources independent of the

Christian Synoptic Gospels that indicate a darkness of three hours.

Mark then continues by stating that after those three hours of darkness Jesus cried out, "My God, my God, why have you deserted me?" Matthew follows the same structure almost word for word. Luke also follows but is the only Gospel writer to add a simple four word explanation for the darkness [chapter 23:45], 'the sun stopped shining.' Was Luke the Gentile coming to the earlier Gospel writings gently challenging the thinking that had developed from the Jewish writers Mark and Matthew? The Gentile mindset was different to that of the Jews and so, perhaps, Luke needed to add a rational statement explaining such a long period of darkness – 'the sun stopped shining' – rather than simply thinking that the darkness was a supernatural intervention by God?

In a traditional interpretation [Borg' 'the old paradigm'], the writers of the four Canonical Gospels were looking back at statements in the Hebrew Scriptures that could indicate the supernatural intervention of God in the life of Jesus by bringing prophecy to fulfilment.

In these four additional words ['the sun stopped shining'] Luke was taking his community back to the great promise of First Isaiah [chapter 9:2]: "The people walking in darkness have seen a great light; on those living in the land of the shadow of death a light has dawned." But I think that Luke was referencing more than the Book of Isaiah. To help his listeners and readers understand how the early Followers of the Way of Jesus felt as they watched their hopes hanging on that broken, dead body on Calvary, Luke may have been referencing the prophet Amos rather than the prophet Isaiah.

"In that day," declares the Sovereign Lord, "I will make the sun go down at noon and darken the earth in broad daylight." [Amos chapter 8:9]: And Luke may have been further referencing the Book of Amos, "He who forms the mountains, creates the wind, and reveals his thoughts to man, he who turns dawn to darkness, and treads the high places of the earth - the LORD God Almighty is his name." [chapter 4:13] to show that the All Powerful God who 'brings darkness at dawn' can also bring darkness at noontime? After all, this is the way in which Midrash works, one writer adding to the texts of previous writers to make more sense of a story for the contemporary times of the writer.

Perhaps Luke was also bringing that sense of the great and terrible Day of Judgment into the events and personalities surrounding the execution of Jesus? If so, perhaps Luke was quoting Joel [chapter 2:31] where the prophet said that "The sun will be turned to darkness and the moon to blood before the coming of the great and dreadful day of the Lord."

Or perhaps Luke was looking back to the prophet Second Isaiah, or if you subscribe to the Three Isaiah scholarship then Third Isaiah, to show that so many people had placed their hope in Jesus but at that moment of execution all seemed lost: "We look for light, but all is darkness; for brightness, but we walk in deep shadows. Like the blind we grope along the wall, feeling our way like men without eyes. At midday we stumble as if it were twilight; among the strong, we are like the dead." [chapter 59:9-10]

Perhaps there was no literal darkness at noon on that awful day at Calvary, but the Gospel writers were metaphorically describing the impact of the noontime events upon the Followers of the Way of Jesus? Could it be that they were all simply saying, "I wasn't there, but this must have been how it felt for the Followers of the Way of Jesus at that moment of his death."

And, remembering that Luke was the Gentile convert to become a Follower of Jesus, perhaps his four-word addition is a commentary upon his later exclusion from the synagogue by those Jews who refused to see Jesus as Messiah? Was this a reflection of Luke's initial struggle with the Jews as he tried to be accepted into the synagogue as a Gentile follower of Jesus? And latterly was Luke reminding those who were being excluded from the synagogue along side him, that their religious Jewish oppressors were actually the losers: "You of this generation, consider the word of the Lord: 'Have I been a desert to Israel or a land of great darkness? Why do my people say, "We are free to roam; we will come to you no more'"? [Jeremiah 2:31] The Jewish Followers of the Way of Jesus had lost their religious heritage by their exclusion from the synagogue, but in Luke's experience of the ongoing presence of the Jesus Spirit, they were the real victors.

Luke's four words, 'the sun stopped shining,' [chapter 23:45], added so much more of the grief and pain felt both by Jesus and his close followers. While not in the least bit detracting from the deep truth of the Mark, Matthew and Luke accounts of the death of Jesus, it makes more sense to me not to interpret these passages as commentary on an actual historic event of a three-hour midday darkness in Jerusalem. Rather, all three Synoptic Gospel writers were telling of the blackness in the hearts and lives of the Followers of the Way of Jesus as they, from a distance, watched him hanging on that cross of execution.

Now comes another statement in that same verse 45 that parallels the other two Synoptic Gospels, "And the curtain of the temple was torn in two." To me, this is the most beautiful, evocative and profound verse in the Christian Scriptures. All three Synoptic Gospels speak of *the* curtain [singular] being torn in two. However, it was in the First Temple, destroyed by the Babylonians in the 6th century B.C.E., that there was a single curtain. This covered a stonewall that separated the Holy of Holies from the Holy Place, the God Presence from the people. Here the High Priest carried out the annual ceremony of repentance during which was the offering of the blood sacrifice that covered the sins of the people. It was in the blood sacrifice that the people believed God forgave their sins.

However, in the time of Jesus it was Herod's Temple, also

known as the Second Temple, that towered over the sacred scenes and structural designs of Jerusalem. In a similar practice to that of the First Temple, only the High Priest on one occasion a year, Yom Kippur or the Day of Atonement, was allowed to go beyond the Holy of Holies into the Holy Place. But in Herod's Temple, there was no stonewall isolating the Holy of Holies from the Holy Place. Instead there were two curtains [Hebrews chapter 9:3, "Behind the second curtain was a room called the Most Holy Place"]. These curtains were each some thirty feet wide and sixty feet high, with a thickness of some three inches. Not surprisingly, each curtain weighed between four and six tons and, according to the Talmud, it took three hundred priests to carry.

There is evidence of an earthquake in 31 C.E. in the Jerusalem area that might have caused the curtain to be ripped apart. Maybe the Synoptic Gospel writers were offering us a majestic description of this amazing historical event but reset it into a different time frame? In my opinion, the earthquake probably did not happen at the exact moment of the execution of Jesus, but in the creative minds of the Synoptic Gospel writers, the earthquake was linked with this later execution of Jesus. Whatever, the impact of his execution and the Truth represented by the torn curtain was a real personal experience for the Synoptic Gospel writers and their communities. The curtain, being torn from the top rather than from the bottom, meant that the tear could not have been the work of a human – it could only have been the work of God. Therefore, as the Synoptic Gospel writers saw it, God had replaced both the curtain and the restricted access of Judaism to God with Jesus. No longer was there the need for a High Priest to perform the duties of Yom Kippur – Jesus was that new High Priest and it was through Jesus, the new Yom Kippur, that all now had direct access to God. This was just as well, because by the time that Matthew and Luke were writing the Temple had been destroyed and the High Priestly role in the Temple had ceased to exist.

No matter how much I have researched the issue, I can find no independent historic evidence to suggest that the curtain of the Temple was torn in this way at the moment when "Jesus called out with a loud voice, 'Father, into your hands I commit my spirit.' When he had said this, he breathed his last." [chapter 23:46]. Whether or not the Synoptic Gospel writers got the timing concerning the tearing of the Temple Curtain and the number of curtains right or wrong is not important. It may have been that the earthquake in 31 C.E. did in fact tear the curtain as history shows that a lintel was dislodged and fell to the ground. But if the curtain had been torn in this way, which curtain would it have been, the outer covering the entrance to the Holy of Holies, or the inner covering the Holy Place? Historically it does not matter but symbolically, in terms of the spiritual content of the story, it had to be the inner curtain that separated all but the High Priest from the presence that was believed to be in the Holy Place.

Even though there may be historical inaccuracies in the chronology of the death of Jesus, the Eternal Truth of the story of the Curtain is what counts – that in Jesus we see and experience the unrestricted Presence of God. This is what Marcus Borg, in his splendid book, *Reading the Bible Again for the First Time* [2001, pp. 50-51], calls 'postcritical naiveté' – even though the story may not be factually true, its Truth, its impact and its meaning are always experientially true! And doubtless, if it had not been torn in 31 C.E., the curtain would have eventually been torn when the Romans destroyed the Temple in 70 C.E. But it is the experience of the symbolism of the Truth contained within the story, rather than the historical accuracy of that story, that really counts.

But note how John's Gospel, the last of our Canon to have been written, approaches the death scene of Jesus. It is just two verses long, [chapter 19: 28 & 29] "Later, knowing that all was now completed, and so that the Scripture would be fulfilled, Jesus said, 'I am thirsty'. A jar of wine vinegar was there, so they soaked a sponge in it, put the sponge on a stalk of the hyssop plant, and lifted it to Jesus' lips. 30 When he had received the drink, Jesus said, 'It is finished'. With that, he bowed his head and gave up his spirit."

"So that the Scripture would be fulfilled" is the clue as to how we should read and interpret the execution stories of Jesus. None of the Gospel writers were writing accurate history. As time went by they were all retelling and adding and fine-tuning the oral stories in answer to more and more questions that were being asked about the purpose and message of Jesus. And the more the questions came, the more the studies of the Hebrew Scriptures offered up prophetic evidence that Jesus was indeed the Messiah, the Christ, the Special Son of God. We should not get hung up on the literalism or otherwise of the Scriptures but, rather, we need to read the Scriptures as wonderful stories but looking for and personally experiencing the Eternal Truth contained within them.

Luke 24:1-12
The Resurrection according to Luke

1 On the first day of the week, very early in the morning, the women took the spices they had prepared and went to the tomb. 2 They found the stone rolled away from the tomb, 3 but when they entered, they did not find the body of the Lord Jesus. 4 While they were wondering about this, suddenly two men in clothes that gleamed like lightning stood beside them. 5 In their fright the women bowed down with their faces to the ground, but the men said to them, "Why do you look for the living among the dead? 6 He is not here; he has risen! Remember how he told you, while he was still with you in Galilee: 7 'The Son of Man must be delivered into the hands of sinful men, be crucified and on the third day be raised again.' 8 Then they remembered his words. 9 When they came back from the tomb, they told all these things to the Eleven and to

all the others. 10 It was Mary Magdalene, Joanna, Mary the mother of James, and the others with them who told this to the apostles. 11 But they did not believe the women, because their words seemed to them like nonsense. 12 Peter, however, got up and ran to the tomb. Bending over, he saw the strips of linen lying by themselves, and he went away, wondering to himself what had happened.

I approach the story of the resurrection of Jesus in a similar manner to that of the Cross and the Temple curtain. If the Bible is the infallible Word of God, without error, why are there so many discrepancies in, arguably, this the most important part of the whole Jesus story? Beginning with Mark's account, the Sabbath day was over when three women, Mary Magdalene, Mary the mother of James, and Salome bought spices for the traditional anointing of a dead body. Although this may have been after nightfall on the Saturday, thus enabling the women to approach the tomb of one who had been executed as a revolutionary troublemaker under cover of darkness, Mark clearly states that the women approached the tomb early the following morning, just after sunrise. However, the timing of this visit would have opened the women to the accusation of being supporters of the executed revolutionary, with all that may have accompanied such a defiant statement. As the three approached the tomb there was concern as to who would roll away the stone that covered the entrance to where the body lay.

However, and for literalists and those who say that there are no errors in Scripture, please note that in Matthew's later account, it is two women, Mary Magdalene and the 'other' Mary, whoever that may have been, who approached the tomb. In Luke's account there is an unspecified number of women who went to the tomb, some of whom are named as Mary Magdalene, Joanna, Mary the mother of James, and the others with them. So how many women actually went to the tomb? Who knows? And when we look at John's account it is one woman alone, Mary Magdalene, who went. So which account of the first day of the week visit to the tomb is the correct version? This is not a pedantic splitting of hairs, but it is a fundamental issue when considering the claimed inerrancy of Scripture.

And things are no clearer as to what happened next. According to Mark, when the women arrived at the tomb they found that the very large stone had been rolled away from the entrance. But Mark offered no explanation as to how this had happened. By the time that Matthew was writing, there had probably been questions as to who was responsible or how the stone had been rolled away, so Matthew offered an answer: there had been a violent earthquake, presumably brought about by an angel of the Lord who had visited from heaven and, not just content to roll the stone away the angel sat on it and waited for the visitors to arrive. However, both Luke and John reverted to Mark's original account and offered no explanation as to how the stone had been rolled away.

The inconsistencies in the accounts did not stop at the entrance to the tomb. Mark has the women entering the tomb and being confronted by the terrifying presence of a young man dressed in a white robe sitting on the right side of the tomb. Why a young man? Why a white robe? Why on the right hand side? Why such detail? Matthew states, rather than just a young man in a white robe, this was the angel whose terrifying appearance was like lightning and his clothes were snow white. But then Luke wrote, not of a young man or an angel, but of two men! Could Luke have misread documents from both Mark and Matthew and used the mathematics of the mad house in which one young man who looked for all the world like the one angel, suddenly became 'one man plus one angel' equals two men? And contrary to all this, according to John, there was no encounter with anyone at the tomb. Mary Magdalene had found the stone at the entrance rolled away and the tomb was empty, and no one, man or angel greeted her.

According to Mark, the young man said, 'Don't be alarmed.' He continued by demonstrating that he had additional information about them and their search by confirming that they were looking for the body of the executed Jesus of Nazareth. The young man then comforted and reassured them by saying, 'He has risen! He is not here. See the place where they laid him.' The young man then issued the heavenly order that they should return to the disciples and to Peter to say that the risen Jesus was going to Galilee to meet with them there. But I wonder why Mark had to name Peter in this way? Perhaps Mark was clearly stating the pre-eminence of Peter as the leader of the Followers of the Way of Jesus at the time when Mark was writing his Gospel in Rome? Perhaps this also indicated Mark's relationship and commitment as the interpreter and supporter of Peter? And perhaps it also indicated rivalry between Peter and, say, James or John for the leadership of the Christian communities at that time?

Only in Matthew's version is there any mention of the guards who were supposedly on duty at the tomb. They, too, were so afraid of the angel that they shook in terror and collapsed. Matthew retells Mark's account almost word for word, as to what the women were told, the invitation into the tomb to see where Jesus had been laid, and the instruction tell the disciples to go to meet with Jesus in Galilee. However, this time there is no especial mention of Peter as there had been in Mark's earlier account.

As so often happened, Luke took the former accounts and added his own spin. The men in the tomb reminded the women of how Jesus, while still with them in Galilee, had told them that it was a deliberate plan that the Son of Man would submit himself to sinners and that he would be crucified but that that would not be the end. The Son of Man would also be raised from death on the third day. Then comes the crux of the whole Luke account, that wonderful question, "Why do you look for the living among the dead?"

As I approach the stories of the resurrection of Jesus this is what warms my Spirit – not the discussion of how many women, men or angels were at the tomb, but the reality of the experience for those earlier Followers of the Way of Jesus, "Why do you look for the living among the dead?"

In my opinion it matters not about the historicity of the resurrection stories. What does matter is the impact of Jesus, executed under Roman authority, who continued to be a living and life-changing presence in the individual and community lives of his Followers.

In John's version, not only are there no others at the tomb, nor is there any instruction to go and tell the disciples to meet with Jesus in Galilee. Notice however what Mark says happened next – the women were trembling and bewildered, and fled from the tomb. And this is critically important, "They said nothing to anyone, because they were afraid." This is where the Gospel of Mark originally ended. At a later date, after Matthew, Luke, John and the Book of Acts had been written, an alternative ending was added in verses 9 and 10. Also there were other endings added to Mark's Gospel: Jesus appearing to Mary Magdalene was copied from Matthew 28:9 and 10; Jesus appearing to two disciples is based upon Luke 24:13-35, the Emmaus Road story; Jesus appearing to the Eleven disciples to instruct them as to what they were to do is taken from Matthew 28:16-20, Luke 24:36-49, John 20:19-23, and Acts 1:6-8; Jesus returning to heaven is based upon stories in both Luke 24:50-53 and Acts 1:9-11.

But Matthew has an entirely different account of what happened next to the women as they left the tomb. This time, although the women were afraid and shaken by the experience at the tomb, they were so full of joy at the encounter and all that it stood for that they ran to inform the disciples as quickly as they possibly could. Are these the same women in both Mark and

Matthew accounts, and if so, who is right in the telling of the story, because both cannot be right? And, in Matthew's account alone, while on their way to tell the disciples the women meet with Jesus. He greets them and they recognize him immediately, falling to the ground to clasp his feet and to worship him.

Luke has none of this meeting with Jesus, but in Luke's version there is the additional little comment, 'they remembered his words.' And they returned to the eleven disciples and to all the other Followers of the Way of Jesus and told them of their experiences at the tomb. But in John's account, Mary Magdalene ran to Peter and one other disciple, 'the one Jesus loved,' to tell them that the body of Jesus had been taken from the tomb. Notice also that she did not go to the eleven.

The response to Mary Magdalene's description of what happened at the tomb must also be considered. Mark says nothing but Matthew has the eleven surviving disciples traveling to a Galilean mountain to meet with Jesus. Between these later additions to Mark's story, Matthew has the sentries taking flight and going to the Chief Priests and leaders to explain what had happened at the tomb. Here are the accounts of the violent earthquake, the angel, the stone that was rolled away, and the disappearance of the body of Jesus. The leaders who had been co-conspirators in the execution of Jesus responded to the story of the guards by commanding them to say to the people, "The disciples of Jesus came during the night and took the body while we were asleep." I am puzzled by this explanation because if this was what really happened, why did they not go to Pilate? Perhaps they were Temple guards rather than Roman guards? But if the latter, why did not Pilate condemn them for neglecting their duties, and sleeping on duty? So be it.

Luke says that the disciples did not believe the details of the women's story, but it was impetuous Peter who decided to run to the tomb to see for himself. However, John takes the fine detail of this Luke version, including the strips of linen cloth, but adds that it was Peter and 'the other disciple' who ran to the tomb. Is there any significance in John having 'the other disciple' getting to the tomb first? Is this the community of John, responsible for the writing of the Gospel credited to John, saying that John was more important than Peter? If so, is this not further evidence, circumstantial may be, of the political infighting and theological differences amongst the various early communities that followed their own interpretations of the teachings of Jesus?

From here on Mark's Gospel is silent and Matthew has little to add. Luke added the stories of the Emmaus Road and the Ascension of Jesus back into heaven. But the encounter between Jesus and Mary Magdalene in Mark 16:9-11, becomes very warm and loving by the time John's Gospel is written. John's Gospel then continued by adding stories that were exclusively its own: the 'confrontation' between Jesus and Doubting Thomas; the materialization of Jesus to seven disciples on the shore of Lake Tiberius; the three questions and follow-up 'feeding' duties from Jesus to Peter; the concluding story in which Jesus gave Peter a new role. But throughout, the writer of John's Gospel maintained that John remained the favorite disciple of Jesus. This again is evidence to me of the rivalry between the followers of Peter's teaching and John's teaching respectively as to who had the authentic message and experience of Jesus!

Finally, there is the exclusive passage that clearly states the reason for the John community writing this Gospel in the first place. It was written 'so that you will put your faith in Jesus as the Messiah and as the Son of God.' This Gospel is the work of an evangelistic community. Historical accuracy was not necessary to communicate the experiential Truth of the continuing presence of the physically dead Jesus. Such was the Truth of their experiences that they could say with maximum confidence, 'In Jesus we have met the fullness of God and you, too, can meet Him and receive life in abundance.'

So, at the end of this analysis of the various and contradictory accounts of what happened to Jesus and his followers after the execution of Jesus, what do I conclude? First that it does not make the slightest bit of difference to me that there was any real historical truth in the post-execution stories. My belief in the rightness of the ways of Jesus of Nazareth, not just for his time but for all time, is not in the least bit shaken by the realization that Jesus was dead, buried and that was the end of the physical body. What I do believe passionately is that the early Followers of the Way of Jesus discovered that as they lived as close as they could to the Perfect Unconditional Love that is God, they experienced the presence of Jesus within themselves and within one another. They explained this reality by using the only words that they had, 'He is risen – he is with us now!'

And that is the Truth for today as well. The truest word in the whole of the Hebrew and Christian Testaments is the word 'Immanuel' for God is indeed with us, within us and about us, inviting us to live the Kingdom of Perfect Unconditional Love here and now. It is the Kingdom life, not for sometime beyond the grave but it is ours to experience at this moment and at every moment.

So does it matter that the resurrection stories of Jesus are not historically or factually true? Not in the least. But by applying Borg's post-critical naivety I can honestly say, 'I know that the Easter experience did not really happen like the confused Gospels tell, but I know that the Easter stories are profoundly true.' And I can experience the Truth of the Easter stories every day in my life and actions and attitudes towards others, in my search of justice and equality for all, and in the struggle to protect this world from the ravages of global warming.

An Easter Truth that does not change me, those around me, and the world in which I live, is a story not worth listening to. But the story of Jesus of Nazareth speaks of the Truth of the God experience like none other. And for that I am eternally grateful.

Luke 24:13-35
On the Road to Emmaus

13 Now that same day two of them were going to a village called Emmaus, about seven miles from Jerusalem. 14 They were talking with each other about everything that had happened. 15 As they talked and discussed these things with each other, Jesus himself came up and walked along with them; 16 but they were kept from recognizing him. 17 He asked them, "What are you discussing together as you walk along?" They stood still, their faces downcast. 18 One of them, named Cleopas, asked him, "Are you only a visitor to Jerusalem and do not know the things that have happened there in these days?"

19 "What things?" he asked. "About Jesus of Nazareth," they replied. "He was a prophet, powerful in word and deed before God and all the people. 20 The chief priests and our rulers handed him over to be sentenced to death, and they crucified him; 21 but we had hoped that he was the one who was going to redeem Israel. And what is more, it is the third day since all this took place. 22 In addition, some of our women amazed us. They went to the tomb early this morning 23 but didn't find his body. They came and told us that they had seen a vision of angels, who said he was alive. 24 Then some of our companions went to the tomb and found it just as the women had said, but him they did not see."

25 He said to them, "How foolish you are, and how slow of heart to believe all that the prophets have spoken! 26 Did not the Christ have to suffer these things and then enter his glory?" 27 And beginning with Moses and all the Prophets, he explained to them what was said in all the Scriptures concerning himself. 28 As they approached the village to which they were going, Jesus acted as if he were going farther. 29 But they urged him strongly, "Stay with us, for it is nearly

evening; the day is almost over." So he went in to stay with them.

30 When he was at the table with them, he took bread, gave thanks, broke it and began to give it to them. 31 Then their eyes were opened and they recognized him, and he disappeared from their sight. 32 They asked each other, "Were not our hearts burning within us while he talked with us on the road and opened the Scriptures to us?" 33 They got up and returned at once to Jerusalem. There they found the Eleven and those with them, assembled together 34 and saying, "It is true! The Lord has risen and has appeared to Simon." 35 Then the two told what had happened on the way, and how Jesus was recognized by them when he broke the bread.

Here in Luke's Emmaus Road story, as they walk despondently towards home, the two are joined by the unrecognized Christ who puts into plain words 'the things about himself in all the Scriptures' so that their hearts were warmed as they listened to this stranger. But this Luke addition raises more questions for me than it offers answers. For example:

- why is it only in Luke's Gospel that there is this story of the meeting on the Emmaus road between these two people and their unrecognized companion?
- why does Luke make this the longest of all the resurrection narratives in the four Gospels?
- why did Cleopas and his unnamed companion not recognize Jesus until the breaking of the bread?
- why did Jesus cease to be the guest in the home of Cleopas when he became the host, taking the bread and breaking it?
- why is it at the moment they recognize him Jesus vanishes from their sight?

But, it is in these and other questions that my understanding of the resurrection of Jesus is summed up. Luke wrote this story to persuade and to educate his readers and listeners that although Jesus had been executed, he was the Lord and the Christ, the long anticipated Son of God, Messiah. In my understanding and interpretation of the Emmaus Road story, the presence of Jesus was not a physical body because a physical body does not materialize and dematerialize at the drop of a hat. The truth for me embedded in this story is that it was the presence of the Spirit of Jesus that the two people experienced on the Emmaus Road.

It is important to remember that it was Paul who probably formulized amongst 'his' early churches around the eastern Mediterranean and Asia Minor, the event that we now call Holy Communion. And here in Luke's writings we again see how the bread and wine had become a central part of the communal life of the Christian communities.

Think again about that Emmaus Road story. It was as the Christ, Risen in the Spirit, took the bread, blessed it, broke it, and shared it with these two that the presence of Jesus was made real to them. It is as we take the bread and wine that we continue as a living part of the same unbroken events of the Easter story.

Life will inevitably present to us at some time enormous sadness and suffering, but the Eternal Truth of the Easter stories is that the spiritually Risen Jesus the Christ is here, indwelling each one of us, constantly partaking with us and encouraging us in the sufferings as we journey down our own Emmaus roads. The Eternal Truth of the Easter stories is that Calvary is always followed by an empty tomb and then comes the joy of the realization of who it is who accompanies us on our Emmaus roads. The Eternal Truth is that when we have to walk our own Emmaus Road it is the same spiritually Risen Jesus the Christ who walked with Cleopas and his companion who both indwells and walks alongside us and shares with us. This is the spiritually Risen Christ of the Emmaus Road; the Christ of all our days that have gone; the Christ of all our todays; the Christ of all our days still to come, who will share with us both in our Calvary pain and in our subsequent joy of the Empty Tomb.

The Eternal Truth of the Easter stories demonstrated so richly in the Emmaus Road story is that no matter how great the pain and the suffering, light will always follow darkness. Our daily task is to look for the indwelling and spiritually Risen Christ constantly coming to us in the most unexpected ways, as the Christ came to these two on the Emmaus Road. Perhaps they were not able to appreciate that their companion was the spiritually Risen Christ because they were not looking for him? Perhaps we suffer from the same short sightedness?

Several years ago, immediately after the morning service, a tramp walked into the Methodist Church in Shenley. He said that he was walking from Luton to London and needed to use the toilet. He did not have the money for the coin operated public toilet in the village. After using the church toilet he was given something to drink and cake to eat, and then my wife and I drove him into Watford to help him find shelter for the night. If the Eternal Truth of Easter really is true, and not some figment of my imagination, then it was in a very real sense the spiritually Risen Christ indwelling that poor man who used the church toilet that morning. And the drink and the cake and the seat in the car were all given to Jesus. The Easter message is that in such simple ways of servant hood we are living the Eternal Truth of the resurrection. To do so will make a difference to us and to those who receive from us.

So, no matter what uncertainties are just ahead of us, we can all live in the Eternal Truth of the Easter stories. The God of coming together and the God of farewells is also the God of constant new beginnings, indwelling each one of us. This is the Presence that will never abandon us or let us down. And as we daily experience, live, serve and trust the spiritually Risen Christ, we will be able to say with the two of them on that

Emmaus road, "Didn't it warm our hearts!"

Summing up comments and reminders.

Biblical scholarship has come on leaps and bounds over the last two hundred years! But sadly many clergy, lay preachers and congregations prefer to ignore these advances wishing to 'leave well alone' and not to have their faith disturbed or, as some see it, distorted by people such as Karen Armstrong, Dietrich Bonhoeffer, Marcus Borg, John Dominic Crossan, Karen King, Elaine Pagels, Paul Tillich, John A T Robinson, Jack Spong, and so on.

This issue is addressed in the lead article in the Newsletter of the Progressive Christianity Network – Britain published in March 2008. In it Brian Wilson writes about recent discussions between the clergy and laity in his parish as they tried to understand the reasons for the decline in church attendance. Wilson writes, "Regrettably, it seemed to be largely a discussion about where to place the deck chairs on the already sinking Titanic, with some of the clergy and most of the laity acting out the part of the band, playing heroically the same old tunes as the ship went down."

Later in the article Wilson writes, "In my worship I find no solace in the dreary banalities and over-busy-ness of modern services, whose language and imagery are largely meaningless to the modern mind.... In our parish discussion, we shied away from any suggestion that the theology we offer is seriously flawed and that the fundamental 'narrative' of faith now lacks credibility for thinking people."

One of Wilson's conclusions is that the decline in church attendance will quicken "if the clergy fail to educate their people in the new insights born of modern science and biblical scholarship."

Biblical scholarship is here to help us, not to hinder us in our journey of faith. Much of what we take for granted as authentic

Christianity does not go back to the historic Jesus who walked on this earth. It goes back to the constant battles between factions of the churches from the time of Jesus right down to today, so that what we have as 'authentic' is no more than the thoughts and experiences of those who won the battles for theological orthodoxy.

We seem to take for granted that the women and men who were the early disciples of Jesus knew, at the end of that first Easter weekend, what we now think we know about Jesus fulfilling the Hebrew Testament prophecies. From reading the Gospel accounts we can know with certainty that immediately after the events of the Cross, the hopes of the disciples were as dead and buried as was Jesus of Nazareth. The Gospel accounts tell us that the terrified followers of Jesus simply locked themselves away as they tried to come to terms with the dashing of their hopes that Jesus was the long awaited Messiah. But the Gospel stories, building upon common sources but written at different times from the seventh to tenth decades of the common era, show us the way in which the theology of Jesus began to develop.

It was a slow process of the pennies dropping, one by one; of question and answer: 'Who was and who is this Jesus who was dead but whom we also experience to be very much part of our lives even though we cannot see him?'

It was a slow process over the ten or fifteen years following that first Easter when the early church leaders in Jerusalem, James the brother of Jesus, Peter and John began to comprehend Jesus as the completion of the Jewish Messianic scriptures.

And into this world of new insights stepped Saul of Tarsus, first persecuting the Followers of the Way of Jesus, and then Saul turned from persecutor to potential rival for the leadership of the growing band of Jesus followers. After his Damascus road experience Saul was transformed into Paul the Apostle, and he began to challenge the exclusive Jewishness of the community of the Followers of Jesus in Jerusalem.

Then as Paul began to take the message of Jesus to other towns and cities around the Mediterranean so Gentiles became Followers of the Way of Jesus without having to become Jews first. Roman persecution and the ill-fated revolt against Rome that, rather than surrender to the tenth legion of the Roman army, concluded with the mass suicide of Jewish fighters and their families at Masada in 73 C.E.

These happenings forced many of the Followers of Jesus out of Jerusalem and new communities became churches as they were, in turn, forced out of the Jewish synagogues in which they had been worshipping the Yahweh God that they had met in Jesus. It was a slow process in which these new early churches began to develop their own understandings of how Jesus of Nazareth had fulfilled the Messianic prophecies of the Jewish Scriptures.

Biblical scholarship informs us that Paul began writing letters to 'his' churches more than a decade before Mark wrote the first Gospel that made it into what became the Christian Testament. Mark's developing theology of Jesus and of God was probably based upon the stories and memories of his companion, the Apostle Peter, and possibly some of the letters of Paul and, although open to debate, other written documents such as the one known as Q and the non-canonical Gospel of Thomas.

Then, after Mark's Gospel came the Gospels of Matthew and Luke. As a primary source, both used Mark's Gospel almost in its entirety but they put their own emphases upon the stories of Mark and then added their own stories including those of the Virgin Birth with the tales of the stable and shepherds and angels and wise men.

There are other very obvious examples of how the later writings of Matthew and Luke and then John demonstrate the developing theology for the different audiences to which they were writing. To begin with, Mark's Gospel infrequently calls Jesus 'Lord' but less than two decades later Luke applies the descriptor 'Lord' to Jesus on seventeen occasions. In fact, Luke emphasizes 'Jesus is Lord' more than any of the other Gospel writers.

Then there are the contradictions within all four Gospel accounts of the Easter Day experiences. The different Gospel stories name different women who went to the Tomb, and in John's Gospel, it was just one woman, Mary Magdalene. When it comes to the resurrection appearances of Jesus, there are further contradictions. Remember that there are no resurrection appearances of Jesus at all in the original manuscripts of Mark's Gospel, only an assurance that Jesus would meet with the disciples in Galilee. Bible scholars mainly agree that Mark chapter 16:9 – 19, telling of the resurrection appearances of Jesus, were probably created and added to later manuscripts.

As the Christian Church faces an uncertain future I am convinced that we who are members of it need to think afresh about how we live; the death of creeds and doctrines; the impact of history remembered, history interpreted and history developed into theology. We cannot continue doing and believing what we seem to have done for centuries, because if we do we will continue to experience what we are going through now, and that is decline. Whatever 'God' is deserves better from us than that.

Postscript

This book has not intentionally tried to undermine the faith journey of any of its readers. What it has tried to do is open up possibilities for a new way forward for individual Followers of the Way of Jesus and for the Churches so that we may find a credible Jesus for the world in which we have to live. There are a hundred or so books and other resources cited at the end of this book. Somewhere within these you will find further possibilities that I hope will invigorate you and your faith.

Appendix

The 1993 Resolutions on Human Sexuality

- The Conference, affirming the joy of human sexuality as God's gift and the place of every human being within the grace of God, recognizes the responsibility that flows from this for us all. It therefore welcomes the serious, prayerful and sometimes costly consideration given to this issue by The Methodist Church.
- All practices of sexuality, which are promiscuous, exploitative or demeaning in any way are unacceptable forms of behavior and contradict God's purpose for us all.
- A person shall not be debarred from church on the grounds of sexual orientation in itself.
- The Conference reaffirms the traditional teaching of the Church on human sexuality; namely chastity for all outside marriage and fidelity within it. The Conference directs that this affirmation is made clear to all candidates for ministry, office and membership, and having established this, affirm that the existing procedures of our church are adequate to deal with all such cases.
- The Conference resolves that its decision in this debate shall not be used to form the basis of a disciplinary charge against any person in relation to conduct alleged to have taken place before such decisions were made.
- Conference recognizes, affirms and celebrates the participation and ministry of lesbians and gay men in the church. Conference calls on the Methodist people to begin a pilgrimage of faith to combat repression and discrimination, to work for justice and human rights and to give dignity and worth to people whatever their sexuality.

Source Material

Allison, Dale C., Borg, Marcus, Crossan, John Dominic, Patterson, Stephen J., *The Apocalyptic Jesus: A Debate*, Polebridge, 2001

Armstrong, Karen, *A History of God*, Ballantine Books, 1993

Armstrong, Karen, *The Battle For God*, Alfred A. Knopf, 2000

Armstrong, Karen, *The Bible: The Biography*, Atlantic Books, 2007

Bartley, J., *The Subversive Manifesto*, Bible Reading Fellowship, 2003

Beck, Brian E., *Christian Character in the Gospel of Luke*, Epworth, 1989

Borg, Marcus, *Jesus: A New Vision*, Harper Collins,1987

Borg, Marcus, *Jesus in Contemporary Scholarship*, Trinity Press International, 1994

Borg, Marcus, *Meeting Jesus Again for the First Time*, Harper Collins,1994

Borg, Marcus, [Ed] *The Lost Gospel Q*, Ulysses Press,1996

Borg, Marcus, *The God We Never Knew*, Harper Collins,1997

Borg, Marcus, & Wright, N.T., *The Meaning of Jesus: Two Visions*, Harper Collins,1999

Borg, Marcus, *Reading the Bible Again for the First Time: Taking the Bible Seriously but Not Literally*, Harper Collins, 2001

Borg, Marcus, *The Heart of Christianity: Rediscovering a Life of Faith*, Harper & Row, 2003

Borg, Marcus, *Jesus: Uncovering the Life, Teachings, and Relevance of a Religious Revolutionary*, Harper Collins, 2006

Borg, Marcus & Scorer, T., *Living the Heart of Christianity: A Guide to Putting Your Faith into Action*, Harper Collins, 2006

Borg, Marcus, & Crossan, John Dominic, *The Last Week: A Day-by-Day Account of Jesus's Final Week in Jerusalem*, Harper Collins, 2006

Borg, Marcus, & Crossan, John Dominic, *The First Christmas: What the Gospels Really Teach About Jesus' Birth*, Harper Collins, 2007

Borg, Marcus, in *Executed by Rome, Vindicated by God, Stricken by God*, ed. by Jersak, B., & Hardin, M, Freshwind Press, 2007

Burklo, J., *Open Christianity*, Rising Star Press, 2000

Chalke, S. & Mann, A., *The Lost Message of Jesus*, Zondervan, 2003

Crossan, John Dominic, *The Dark Interval*, Polebridge, 1994

Crossan, John Dominic, *In Parables*, Polebridge, 1994

Crossan, John Dominic, *Jesus: A Revolutionary Biography*, Harper Collins, 1995

Crossan, John Dominic, *God and Empire: Jesus Against Rome, Then and Now*, Harper Collins, 2007

Dawes, Hugh, *Freeing the Faith: A Credible Christianity for Today*, SPCK, 1992

De Chardin, T. *The Phenomenon of Man*, Harper Torchbooks, The Cloister Library, Harper & Row, 1961

Dodd, C. H., *The Parables of the Kingdom*. [rev. ed.], Scribner, 1961

Funk, R.W., *A Credible Jesus: Fragments of a Vision*, Polebridge, 2002

Grant, R.M. & Freedmand, D.N., *The Secret Sayings of Jesus*, Fontana, 1960

Harpur, T. *The Pagan Christ*, Thomas Allen Publishers, 2004

Holloway, Richard, *Doubts and Loves: What is Left of Christianity*, Canongate Books, 2001

Jeremias, Joachim. *The Parables of Jesus*. 2d rev. ed., Scribner. 1972

King, Karen L., *Gospel of Mary Magdala*, Polebridge, 2003

King, Karen L., *What is Gnosticism?* Belknap Press, 2005

Lieu, Judith, *The Gospel of Luke*, Epworth, 1997

Lynch, G., *The New Spirituality*, I.B. Tauris, 2007

Mack, Burton, *The Lost Gospel: The Book of Q & Christian Origins*, Harper Collins, 1993

Marsh, C., *Christianity in a Post-Atheist Age*, SCM, 2002

Marshall, I.Howard, *Luke – Historian and Theologian*, Paternoster, 1970

Pagels, E., *The Gnostic Gospels*, Vintage Books, 1989

Pagels, E., *Beyond Belief: The Secret Gospel of Thomas*, Vintage

Books, 2003

Patterson, Stephen J., *Q-Thomas Reader*, Polebridge, 1990

Robinson, John A.T., *Honest to God*, SCM, 1963

Sacks, J., *The Dignity of Difference*, Continuum, 2002

Sahajananda, J. M., *Hindu Christ*, O Books, 2006

Sanders, E.P., *The Historical Figure of Jesus*, Penguin, 1993

Spong, John Shelby, *Living in Sin? A Bishop Rethinks Human Sexuality*, Harper Collins, 1988

Spong, John Shelby, *Rescuing the Bible from Fundamentalism: A Bishop Rethinks the Meaning of Scripture*, Harper Collins, 1991

Spong, John Shelby, *Born of a Woman: A Bishop Rethinks the Birth of Jesus*, Harper Collins, 1992

Spong, John Shelby, *Resurrection: Myth or Reality? A Bishop's Search for the Origins of Christianity*, Harper Collins, 1994

Spong, John Shelby, *Liberating the Gospels: Reading the Bible with Jewish Eyes*, Harper Collins, 1996

Spong, John Shelby, *Why Christianity Must Change or Die: A Bishop Speaks to Believers In Exile*, Harper Collins, 1999

Spong, John Shelby, *Here I Stand: My Struggle for a Christianity of Integrity, Love and Equality*, Harper Collins, 2001

Spong, John Shelby, *A New Christianity for a New World: Why Traditional Faith Is Dying and How a New Faith Is Being Born*, Harper Collins, 2002

Spong, John Shelby, *The Sins of Scripture: Exposing the Bible's Texts of Hate to Reveal the God of Love*, Harper Collins, 2005

Spong, John Shelby, *Jesus for the Non-Religious*, Harper Collins, 2007

Theissen, G., *The New Testament*, Continuum Imprint, 2003

Tillich, Paul, *The Shaking of the Foundations*, Pelican, 1962

Vermes, G., *The Dead Sea Scrolls in English*, Pelican, 1962

Vermes, G, *Jesus the Jew*, SCM, 2001

Wallis, J., *The Soul of Politics*, Harper Collins, 1994

Wallis, J., *Faith Works*, SPCK, 2002

Suggested Further Reading

Adams, James, R., *From Literal to Literary*, Rising Star Press, 2005

Allen, C., *The Human Christ: The Search for the Historical Jesus*, Lion, 1998

Bultmann, Rudolf, *Jesus and the Word*, Collins Fontana, 1958

Burrows, P.M., *Gospel of Doubt*, Pentland Press, 1998

Clements, K.W., *Friedrich Schleiermacher*, Collins, 1987

Cupitt, Don, *After God: The Future of Religion*, Phoenix, 1998

Cupitt, Don, *Taking leave of God*, SCM, 2001

Cupitt, Don, *The Sea of Faith*, SCM, 2003

Davie, G., *Religion in Modern Europe*, Oxford University, 2000

Davie, G., *Europe: The Exceptional Case – Parameters of Faith in the Modern World*, Darton, Longman & Todd, 2002

Dawkins, R., *The God Delusion*, Black Swan, 2007

Field, F., *The Politics of Paradise*, Collins Fount, 1987

Forward, M., [Ed], *Ultimate Visions*, Oneworld, 1995

Forward, M., *Jesus: A Short Biography*, Oneworld, 1998

Freeman, Anthony, *God in us: A case for Christian Humanism*, Imprint Academic, 2nd ed., 2001

Heath, G, *Believing in Nothing and Something*, Bowland Press, 2003

Jenkins, David, *The Calling of a Cuckoo: Not Quite an Autobiography*, Continuum, 2002

Lee, M., *Written in Jest*, Robson, 2002

Moltman, Jurgen, *Theology and Joy*, SCM, 1973

Newman, J., *Foundations of Religious Tolerance*, University of Toronto Press, 1982

Robinson, John A.T., *The New Reformation?* SCM, 1965

Robinson, John A.T., *But That I Can't Believe*, Collins Fontana, 1967

Schonfield, H., *The Essene Odyssey*, Element Books, 1984

Smith, A.B., *A New Framework for Christian Belief*, O Books, 2002

Smith, A.B., *The Creative Christian*, O Books, 2006

Tomlinson, D., *The Post Evangelical*, SPCK, 1995

Wallis, J., *The New Radical*, Lion, 1983

Ward, Tess, *The Celtic Wheel of the Year*, O Books, 2007

Williams, Rowan, *Resurrection*, Darton, Longman & Todd, 1982

Williams, Rowan, *On Christian Theology*, Blackwell, 2000

DVDs
Living the Questions, 2005, www.livingthequestions.com

Saving Jesus, 2006, www.livingthequestions.com

Eclipsing Empire, 2008, www.livingthequestions.com

Internet Resources
Asbury United Methodist Church, Phoenix, Arizona.
   www.aplaceforallpeople.com

Borg, Marcus, www.marcusborg.com

Center for Progressive Christianity in America, www.tcpc.org

Canadian Center for Progressive Christianity.
   www.progressivechristianity.ca

Christ Community Church, Spring Lake, Michigan
   www.christ-community.net

Crossan, John Dominic, www.johndcrossan.com

Free to Believe, www.freetobelieve.org.uk

North East Valley Baptist Church, Dunedin, New Zealand.
   www.valleybaptist.org.nz

Practical Dreamers, Dunedin Methodist Church, New Zealand.
   www.dunedinmethodist.org.nz

Progressive Christianity Network – Britain,
   www.pcnbritain.org.uk

Rex Hunt, http://rexaehuntprogressive.com

Spiritual But Not Religious [SBNR], SBNR.org

Spirited Exchanges, www.spiritedexchanges.org.nz

Spong, John Shelby, www.johnshelbyspong.com

Westar Institute/Jesus Seminar, www.westarinstitute.org

B O O K S

O is a symbol of the world, of oneness and unity. In different cultures it also means the "eye," symbolizing knowledge and insight. We aim to publish books that are accessible, constructive and that challenge accepted opinion, both that of academia and the "moral majority."

Our books are available in all good English language bookstores worldwide. If you don't see the book on the shelves ask the bookstore to order it for you, quoting the ISBN number and title. Alternatively you can order online (all major online retail sites carry our titles) or contact the distributor in the relevant country, listed on the copyright page.

See our website www.o-books.net for a full list of over 500 titles, growing by 100 a year.

And tune in to myspiritradio.com for our book review radio show, hosted by June-Elleni Laine, where you can listen to the authors discussing their books.

mySpiritRadio